4-Step Chicken Recipes

Sterling Publishing Co., Inc.
New York

Library of Congress Cataloging-in-Publication Data Available

10 9 8 7 6 5 4 3 2

Published by Sterling Publishing Co., Inc.
387 Park Avenue South, New York, NY 10016
Originally published in Canada in 2002 by
Éditions TOTAL Publishing under the title *4 Steps Chicken Recipes*
© 2002 by Éditions TOTAL Publishing

Sterling ISBN 1-4027-0730-4

Contents

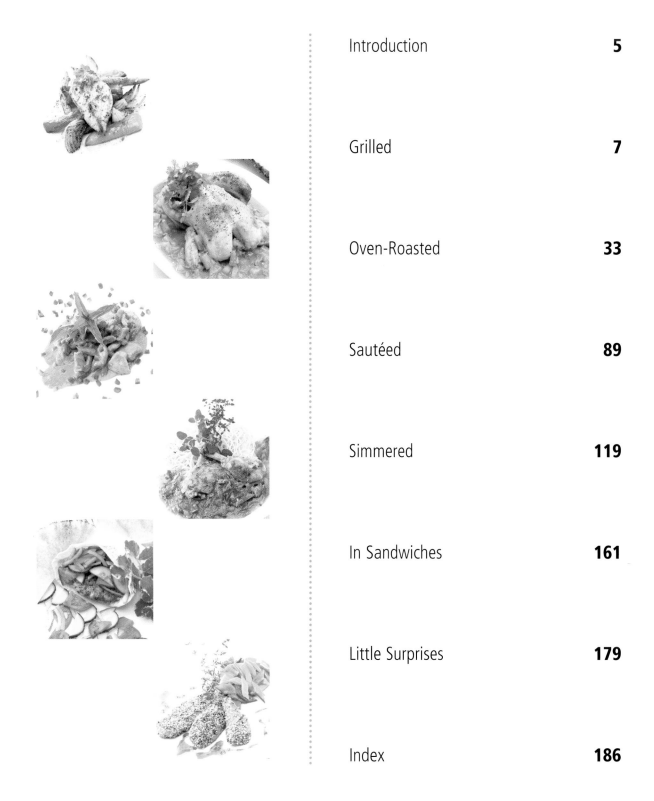

Introduction

Nowadays, eating well isn't as easy as one would think. Our overloaded schedules leave us little time for cooking. We are eating more and more frozen, tasteless, prepackaged meals than ever before, or else we choose fast food restaurants, which do not serve very well-balanced meals. We also lack inspiration when it comes to planning and varying our menus.

With its modern and dynamic approach, the **4-Step Cooking Collection** offers welcome solutions on how to quickly prepare dishes that are both tasty and nourishing. Come and discover the joys of delicious eating with every turn of the page. The recipes presented in this collection are easy to prepare. Each recipe is broken down into 4 easy steps, no more, no less. What's more, most of these recipes use ingredients that you will find in your local grocery store, thus helping you to save unnecessary time running around. Now eating well is as easy as 1-2-3… 4! Good ingredients, clear and precise instructions, a few "culinary secrets," that's all you need to surprise your guests. You are never more than 4 Steps away from your next delicious meal!

Chicken can be easily found on the market throughout the year, and is available in a variety of useful cuts. It is no longer necessary to sharpen your cleaver and pretend to be a surgeon if you are looking for boneless chicken breasts, as they are already prepared for you and ready in your grocer's display case.

All the chicken recipes presented here are prepared in 4 steps. Whether they are famous classic recipes (adapted to today's tastes) or modern and exotic recipes, they have all been conceived for their ease and rapidity of execution. Four easy steps to follow and you will be serving an excellent meal at the dinner table, one which is tastier and more satisfying.

You will be surprised to learn about the wide range of dishes that can be made with chicken: sauce-covered dishes with deliciously aromatic fragrances, crispy morsels that will make your mouth water, as well as tasty salads. Grilled, sautéed, oven-roasted or simmered, chicken remains a dinner table favorite. And you don't have to tell anyone that you prepared the meal just by counting to 4!

Cajun Chicken Wings with Garlic

4 SERVINGS

2 tbsp	vegetable oil
3	garlic cloves, finely chopped
2 tbsp	Cajun seasoning
	juice of 1 lemon
12	chicken wings, cut in half
½ cup	sour cream
3	green onions, finely chopped
	salt and freshly ground pepper, to taste

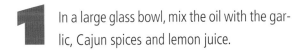

1 In a large glass bowl, mix the oil with the garlic, Cajun spices and lemon juice.

2 Toss the chicken wings in the garlic Cajun mixture. Cover and marinate in the refrigerator for at least 2 hours.

3 Meanwhile in a small bowl, mix the sour cream and the green onions and season to taste with salt and pepper. Cover and refrigerate until ready to serve.

4 Preheat the barbecue grill or preheat the oven to 400°F and grill or bake the chicken wings, turning often, for 10 to 20 minutes, until crisp and cooked through. Serve with the sour cream dip.

Grilled

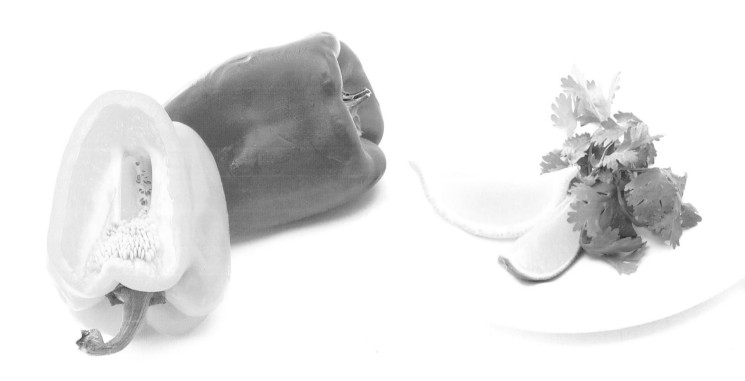

Grilled Chicken and Vegetables

4 SERVINGS

Chicken

4	skinned, bone-in chicken breast halves
1	red pepper, quartered
1	yellow pepper, quartered
1	Spanish onion, quartered
12	canned baby corn

Marinade

⅓ cup	olive oil
	juice of 1 lime
	juice of 1 lemon
1	hot chile pepper, chopped
1	garlic clove, minced
1 tsp	ground coriander
	salt and freshly ground pepper, to taste
	fresh cilantro or parsley sprigs (garnish)
	lime quarters (garnish)
	lemon quarters (garnish)

1 Place the chicken breasts and vegetables in a 13 x 9 in. glass baking dish.

2 In a small bowl, mix together the olive oil, lime and lemon juice, the chile pepper, and the garlic and coriander. Season to taste with salt and pepper and pour over the chicken breasts and vegetables. Turn to coat. Cover and marinate in the refrigerator for 2 hours.

3 Discard the marinade. Preheat the barbecue grill to high. Grill the chicken breasts and vegetables for 10 to 15 minutes, turning often, until the vegetables are tender and the chicken cooked through.

4 Garnish with fresh cilantro or parsley, and the lime and lemon quarters.

Note
Use a grill rack for the baby corn or tread them on metal skewers so they don't fall through the grates of the grill.

Grilled

Grilled Curry Chicken

4 SERVINGS

Chicken

1   whole chicken
(3¼ lb)

     salt and freshly ground pepper, to taste

Marinade

½ cup   vegetable oil

2 tbsp   curry powder

2 tbsp   honey

2 tbsp   lemon juice

1 tbsp   chopped garlic

1 tbsp   chopped fresh ginger

1 tsp   ground nutmeg

1 tsp   crushed red pepper flakes

1 tsp   ground cumin

1 tsp   ground turmeric

1 Cut the chicken into 8 pieces and prick all over with a fork.

2 In a large glass bowl, mix all the marinade ingredients together.

3 Place the chicken pieces in the marinade and turn to coat well. Cover and marinate in the refrigerator for 24 hours.

4 Preheat the barbecue grill to medium. Season with salt and pepper to taste, if desired. Grill the chicken for 30 minutes, turning frequently, until cooked through. Serve hot or at room temperature.

Note

Serve with a curry sauce. Prepare a white sauce from a mix and add a pinch each of the same spices in the marinade.

Grilled

Triple-flavored Yakitori

4 SERVINGS

Marinade

1 cup	sake or dry white wine
½ cup	soy sauce
½ cup	mirin (mild rice wine) (optional)
3 tbsp	honey
1 tbsp	grated fresh ginger

Chicken

2	skinless, boneless chicken breast halves
16	large shrimp, peeled, tails left on
16	sea scallops
1 tbsp	sesame seeds

1 In a heavy medium saucepan, mix all the marinade ingredients together. Bring to a boil over medium heat and let simmer for 15 minutes. Remove from the heat and let cool. Transfer to a bowl and cover with plastic wrap; refrigerate.

2 On a work surface, cut the chicken breasts into 16 chunks. Place in a bowl and cover with ⅓ of the marinade. Butterfly the shrimps by splitting them through the center lengthwise with a sharp knife. Place the shrimps and scallops in the remaining marinade. Cover both bowls and marinate in the refrigerator for approximately 1 hour.

3 Thread 8 metal or wooden skewers evenly with the chicken strips, shrimps and scallops. Discard the marinade.

4 Preheat the barbecue grill to medium. Grill the brochettes (yakitori) until the chicken and seafood are cooked through, turning frequently. Sprinkle with the sesame seeds and serve hot, accompanied with rice.

Grilled

Grilled Chicken Fillets
and Vegetables

4 SERVINGS

Chicken

8   chicken tenders
(3½ oz each)

Marinade

3 tbsp   teriyaki sauce

1 tbsp   julienne-cut fresh ginger

1   red pepper, cut in large strips

1   green pepper, cut in large strips

2   tomatoes, quartered

1   onion, cut into six wedges

1   small eggplant, cut in 1 in rounds

2 tbsp   olive oil

       salt and frshly ground pepper, to taste

Sauce

½ cup   plain yogurt

1 tbsp   chicken broth granules

3 tbsp   sunflower seeds

1 Place the chicken tenders in a shallow glass dish, and add the teriyaki sauce and the ginger. Cover and marinate for 1 hour in the refrigerator.

2 Preheat a large stovetop grill pan over medium heat. Oil the pan lightly. Drain the chicken tenders. Pan-grill, turning once, for 8 minutes, until cooked through. Transfer to a platter and cover to keep warm.

3 Place the vegetables, oil and salt and pepper to taste in a large bowl. Mix well. Grill, in batches, until tender and lightly charred. Transfer to the platter with the chicken.

4 In a small bowl, mix the yogurt and chicken broth granules until blended. Stir in the sunflower seeds. Serve the sauce with the chicken and vegetables.

Grilled

Mini Brochettes with 2 Flavors

20 BROCHETTES

Chicken

6	skinless, boneless chicken breast halves
20	wooden skewers

Marinade 1

2 tbsp	soy sauce
1 tbsp	teriyaki sauce
1 tsp	grated fresh ginger

Marinade 2

½ cup	dry white wine
⅓ cup	miso paste
	or
2 tbsp	chicken broth granules

Sauce

	juice of 1 orange
⅓ cup	pineapple juice
1 tbsp	beef broth granules
½ tsp	cornstarch, mixed with 1 tsp cold water
2 tbsp	thinly sliced green onion

1 Cut the chicken into 20 strips, and thread onto the wooden skewers.

2 In a shallow dish, mix together the ingredients of the first marinade, and arrange half the chicken brochettes in this mixture. In another dish, mix the ingredients for the second marinade, and place the remaining skewers in this marinade. Cover both dishes and marinate overnight in the refrigerator.

3 Preheat the barbecue grill to medium. In a small saucepan, bring the orange and pineapple juice and broth granules to a boil. Simmer for 2 minutes over low heat. Stir in the cornstarch mixture and cook, stirring, until thickened. Add the green onion, remove from heat and keep warm.

4 Drain the brochettes and grill, turning once, for 4 to 6 minutes, until cooked through. Pour the sauce into a small bowl and serve with the brochettes.

Grilled

Chicken Liver Brochettes

4 SERVINGS

Chicken Livers

3	slices bacon
8	pitted prunes
1 lb	chicken livers
1	red pepper, cut in squares
1	onion, cut in squares
8	baby dill pickles

Marinade

2 tbsp	light corn syrup
1 tbsp	grated fresh ginger
1	garlic clove, chopped
2 tbsp	tamari or soy sauce
1 tbsp	ketchup

1 Place the bacon on paper towels and microwave on high (100%) for 2 minutes. Cut the bacon slices in three and wrap each prune with a piece of the bacon. Trim the chicken livers, and cut into chunks.

2 In a shallow dish, mix all the marinade ingredients together and set aside.

3 Thread 8 skewers, alternating with 1 piece of red pepper, 1 chicken liver, 1 bacon-wrapped prune, 1 piece of onion, and finish with a pickle. Place in the marinade, turn to coat, cover and marinate for 30 minutes in the refrigerator.

4 Preheat the barbecue grill to medium. Oil the grids. Grill the brochettes, turning once, for 5 to 8 minutes, until the chicken liver is cooked. Serve hot with rice.

Grilled

Marinated Chicken Breasts

4 SERVINGS

Marinade

¼ cup	lemon juice
¼ cup	dry white wine or apple juice
1	package of dehydrated onion soup mix
1 tbsp	vegetable oil
1 tsp	dried basil

Chicken

4	skinless chicken breast halves (boned or bone in)

1 In a shallow glass dish, combine the lemon juice, white wine or apple juice, the onion soup, vegetable oil and the basil.

2 Add the chicken to this marinade, turn to coat, and set aside for 20 minutes, turning occasionally.

3 Preheat the barbecue grill to medium-high. Oil the grids. Remove the chicken from the marinade (reserve the marinade).

4 Grill the chicken, turning once, and basting twice with the marinade for about 15 minutes, until the chicken is cooked through. Discard any remaining marinade.

Grilled

Chicken Brochettes
with Yogurt Sauce

4 SERVINGS

½ cup	plain yogurt
¼ cup	chopped fresh parsley
¼ cup	dry white wine
	juice of 1 lemon
2 tbsp	chopped fresh oregano
1 tbsp	garlic powder
	salt and freshly ground pepper, to taste
4	skinless, boneless chicken breast halves cubed
4	wooden skewers

1 In a small bowl, combine all the ingredients except the chicken. Mix well.

2 Thread the chicken cubes onto the skewers, arrange in a large glass dish and cover with half of the sauce. Cover and marinate in the refrigerator for 2 hours, turning occasionally. Drain.

3 Preheat the barbecue or a stovetop grill pan. Oil the grids (or the pan). Grill, turning 2 or 3 times, until chicken is cooked through.

4 Serve the remaining sauce over the brochettes.

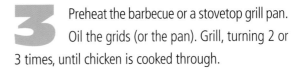

Grilled

Trio on the Grill

4 SERVINGS

¼ cup	dry white wine
1 tbsp	vegetable oil
2	garlic cloves, finely chopped
1 tsp	Dijon mustard
	pepper, to taste
16	chicken wings, halved, or 8 drumsticks
16	large shrimp, peeled and deveined
16	large sea scallops

Sauce

1 cup	plain yogurt
½ cup	peeled, seeded and coarsely chopped cucumber
1	garlic clove, coarsely chopped
	salt and freshly ground pepper, to taste
	Croutons
8	bread slices, crusts removed
1 tbsp	vegetable oil

1 In a large glass bowl, mix together the wine, oil, garlic, mustard and pepper. Toss the chicken wings or drumsticks, shrimp and the scallops in this marinade. Cover and marinate for 3 hours in the refrigerator. Thread 2 shrimps and 2 scallops on each of 8 small wooden or metal skewers.

2 Using a food processor, blend the yogurt, cucumber and garlic until smooth and creamy. Season to taste with salt and pepper; set aside.

3 Preheat the barbecue grill to medium-high. Grill the chicken wings or drumsticks, turning often for 15 to 25 minutes (respectively). Grill the skewers for 3 to 4 minutes each side, basting with the marinade during cooking. Discard the remaining marinade.

4 Meanwhile, using a rolling pin, flatten the bread slices into fine sheets, cut with a round cookie cutter and oil lightly. Lightly toast the bread circles, scoring them on the grill. Place the chicken wings or drumsticks and the skewers on top of the bread circles on a serving plate, top with the sauce and serve.

Grilled

Tandoori Chicken Wings
with Mint

2 SERVINGS

Marinade

¼ cup	plain yogurt
1 tbsp	white vinegar
1	garlic clove, chopped
2 tsp	ground cumin
2 tsp	ground turmeric
1 tsp	ground coriander
1 tsp	paprika
½ tsp	ground ginger
12	chicken wings, halved

Sauce

½ cup	plain yogurt
1 tbsp	honey
½ tsp	chopped fresh mint

1 In a small bowl, mix all the marinade ingredients together, and pour into a shallow dish.

2 Place the chicken wings in the dish with the marinade and turn several times to thoroughly coat them with the mixture. Cover and marinate for approximately 8 hours in the refrigerator.

3 In a small bowl, mix together the yogurt, honey and the mint; cover and refrigerate until ready to serve.

4 Preheat the barbecue grill to medium. Grill the wings, turning often, until crisp and cooked through. Serve with the yogurt sauce.

Grilled

Grilled Chicken with Curry Sauce

4 SERVINGS

Chicken

1	whole chicken
(3 lb)	
	salt and freshly ground pepper, to taste

Marinade

½ cup	vegetable oil
2 tbsp	curry powder
2 tbsp	lemon juice
2 tbsp	honey
1 tbsp	chopped garlic
1 tbsp	chopped fresh ginger
1 tsp	crushed red pepper
1 tsp	ground nutmeg
1 tsp	ground cumin
1 tsp	ground turmeric

1 Cut the chicken into 8 pieces and prick all over with a fork.

2 In a large glass bowl, mix all the marinade ingredients together.

3 Place the chicken pieces in the marinade and turn to coat. Cover and marinate in the refrigerator for 24 hours.

4 Preheat the barbecue grill to medium. Season the chicken with salt and pepper to taste. Grill for approximately 40 minutes, turning the pieces frequently, until cooked through. Serve hot or at room temperature.

Grilled

Tandoori Chicken Supremes

6 SERVINGS

6	skinned, bone-in chicken breast halves **(4 oz each)**
⅔ cup	plain yogurt
½ cup	vegetable oil
	juice of 3 lemons
4	garlic cloves, crushed
1 tbsp	paprika
2 tsp	ground cumin
2 tsp	ground turmeric
2 tsp	chicken broth granules
½ tsp	ground ginger
	lemon quarters (garnish)

1 Cut shallow incisions in the chicken breasts and place them in a 13 x 9 in. glass baking dish.

2 In a medium bowl, combine the yogurt, oil, lemon juice, garlic, paprika, cumin, turmeric, broth granules and ginger. Mix well.

3 Pour this mixture over the chicken breasts and turn to coat well. Cover and marinate in the refrigerator for 12 hours. Drain the chicken, reserving the marinade.

4 Preheat the barbecue grill to medium. Oil the grids. Grill the chicken, turning once, for approximately 10 minutes each side, brushing often with the marinade, until the chicken is cooked through. Serve hot with rice, garnished with lemon quarters.

Grilled

Light Honey Chicken

4 SERVINGS

4	skinless, boneless chicken breast halves
2 tbsp	all-purpose flour
1 tbsp	vegetable oil
1 tbsp	butter
2 tbsp	grated lemon zest
2 tbsp	honey
2 tbsp	water
2 tbsp	chicken broth granules
	pinch of dried marjoram (or 1 tbsp chopped fresh marjoram)
	salt and freshly ground pepper, to taste

1 Preheat the oven to 350°F. Lightly flour the chicken. In a large nonstick skillet, heat the oil and butter over medium heat. Add the chicken and brown on both sides, approximately 5 minutes.

2 Place the chicken in an ovenproof dish and transfer to the oven. Bake for 10 minutes (or more, depending on the size of the breasts), until cooked through. Remove from the oven.

3 Discard any drippings from the skillet. Add the lemon zest, honey, water, chicken broth granules and marjoram, and season to taste with salt and pepper. Cook, stirring, over very low heat until the mixture begins to boil.

4 Then add the chicken and turn to coat well with the pan juices before serving.

Note

For a more festive look, julienne the lemon zest instead of grating it. First remove the brightly colored part of the peel with a vegetable peeler, then use a sharp knife to cut it into shreds.

Oven-Roasted

Poultry Ballotines with Fruit Pilaf

4 SERVINGS

Fruit Pilaf

½ cup	brown rice
	hot water
1 tsp	vegetable oil
½ cup	chopped onions
1 cup	chicken broth
2 tsp	soy sauce
1	peach, peeled, pitted, and cut in small cubes
1	apple, peeled, cored and cut in small cubes
¼ cup	raisins
1 tsp	grated fresh ginger
	salt and freshly ground pepper, to taste

Chicken

| 4 | large skinless, boneless chicken breast halves |
| | salt and freshly ground pepper, to taste |

Sauce

1	medium onion, finely chopped
½ cup	dry white wine
2 tsp	cornstarch mixed with 1 tbsp cold water
1½ cups	chicken broth
1 tsp	paprika
1 tsp	fresh lemon juice
	salt and freshly ground pepper, to taste

1 Preheat the oven to 350°F. Place the rice in a bowl and cover with hot water; let soak for 20 minutes, rinse in cold water and drain. In a medium oven proof saucepan, heat the oil over medium heat and sauté the rice with the onion for 2 minutes, stirring. Add the rest of the pilaf ingredients. Bring to a boil, cover and cook 20 minutes, until tender. Set aside to cool.

2 Preheat the oven to 350°F. With a sharp knife, cut open a pocket lengthwise in the chicken breasts. Season with salt and pepper, and stuff them with the fruit pilaf. Secure the open sides with toothpicks. Place them in a buttered pie plate, cover with foil and bake for 20 minutes; until cooked through. Remove and set aside for 10 minutes, covered.

3 Meanwhile, in a medium saucepan, combine the onion and the wine. Simmer over medium heat until reduced by half. Add the chicken broth and paprika. Simmer over low heat for 20 minutes. Add the cornstarch mixture and cook, stirring, until thickened.

4 Add the lemon juice and salt and pepper to taste to the sauce. Slice the ballotines at an angle, arrange on plates and coat with the sauce.

Oven-Roasted

Chicken Sausages
with Creamy Mustard Sauce

4 SERVINGS

Chicken Sausages

1 lb	ground chicken
1½ tsp	rubbed sage
½ tsp	garlic powder
½ tsp	onion powder
½ tsp	ground nutmeg
	pinch of ground cinnamon
	pinch of ground cloves
	salt and freshly ground pepper, to taste
1 tbsp	butter

Creamy Mustard Sauce

1 cup	sour cream
2 to 3 tbsp	heavy or light cream
4 tsp	Dijon mustard
¼ tsp	dry mustard
	salt and freshly ground pepper, to taste

1 Preheat the oven to 350°F. Using a food processor, thoroughly mix together all the sausage ingredients. Divide the mixture into 4 parts and shape into 1 to 1¼ in. diameter sausages.

2 In a large nonstick ovenproof skillet, melt the butter over medium heat. Brown the chicken sausages. Transfer to the oven and bake for approximately ten minutes, until cooked through.

3 In a small bowl, whisk together the sour cream and heavy or light cream, the Dijon mustard and dry mustard and season to taste with salt and pepper.

4 Place a bit of the creamy mustard sauce on each plate and dress with the sliced chicken sausages.

Oven-Roasted

Chicken Tournedos with Apple

4 SERVINGS

¼ cup	wild rice
2½ cups	apple juice
	salt and freshly ground pepper, to taste
1	green apple, cored and cut in small cubes
¼ cup	diced carrot, blanched
4	large skinless, boneless chicken breast halves
2 tbsp	all-purpose flour
2 tbsp	butter
¾ cup	prepared chicken gravy
2 tbsp	heavy cream
	rosemary sprigs (garnish)

1 In a small saucepan, combine the wild rice and the apple juice, seasoning to taste with salt and pepper. Cover and cook over high heat for 50 minutes, stirring often, until the rice is tender.

2 Drain the wild rice, reserving the cooking juice. Add the apple cubes and diced carrot to the rice. Season to taste, cover to keep warm and set aside. Preheat the oven to 350°F.

3 Season the chicken with salt and pepper and dust with flour. In a large nonstick skillet, melt the butter over medium-high heat. Add the chicken and cook for 5 minutes, turning once, until browned. Transfer to a pie plate and bake for 8 minutes, until cooked through.

4 Discard the drippings from the skillet. Add the chicken gravy, cream and reserved rice cooking juice. Cook, stirring over medium heat, until thickened and bubbly. Serve the chicken with the rice. Garnish with rosemary sprigs.

Note

Wild rice is nutritious and rich in fiber, and quadruples in volume when cooked.

Oven-Roasted

Chicken Pockets

4 SERVINGS

4	large skinless, boneless chicken breast halves
1 tbsp	vegetable oil
	salt and freshly ground pepper, to taste
1 bag	spinach, slightly cooked and drained
8 slices	mozzarella cheese
1 tbsp	butter
1	shallot, chopped
1 tbsp	chopped fresh garlic
⅓ cup	dry white wine
1 can **(14½ oz)**	diced tomatoes with herbs, drained and pureed to a chunky texture
1 cup	prepared chicken gravy
	salt and freshly ground pepper, to taste

1 Preheat the oven to 350°F. Cut each chicken breast in half lengthwise. Flatten the slices gently. In a large nonstick skillet, heat the oil over medium-high heat. Cook the chicken 2 minutes on each side. Season with salt and pepper.

2 Top 4 chicken pieces with the spinach and 2 cheese slices each. Cover these with the remaining four chicken pieces, letting the cheese overlap. Arrange on a greased jelly-roll pan and bake for 10 minutes until the cheese has melted. Remove and keep warm.

3 In the same skillet, melt the butter over medium heat. Sauté the shallots and the garlic. Add the white wine and boil for 2 minutes. Add the tomatoes and the chicken gravy. Bring to a boil. Lower the heat and let simmer for 12 minutes, until slightly thickened. Season with salt and pepper.

4 Coat serving plates with the sauce and arrange the chicken pockets on top. Accompany with pasta and fresh vegetables.

Oven-Roasted

Chicken Supremes in Mustard

4 SERVINGS

1 tbsp	Dijon mustard
1 tbsp	honey
1 tbsp	tomato paste
½ cup	plain dry bread crumbs
¼ tsp	ground cayenne pepper
1 tsp	paprika
½ tsp	celery salt
4	skinless, boneless chicken breast halves

1 Preheat the oven to 350°F. In a medium bowl, mix together the mustard, honey and tomato paste.

2 In a pie plate, mix together the breadcrumbs and spices.

3 Coat each chicken breast with the mustard mixture and dredge in the spiced breadcrumbs, pressing so they adhere.

4 Place the chicken breasts in a greased baking dish and bake at 350° for 50 minutes. Let stand for 5 minutes and serve.

Oven-Roasted

Sicilian Chicken

4 SERVINGS

1 lb	skinless, boneless chicken breasts, cut in strips
3 tbsp	all-purpose flour
3 tbsp	olive oil
1	onion, chopped
2	garlic cloves, chopped
2 cups	chicken broth
1 can (14½ oz)	diced tomatoes, with juice
½ cup	whole Sicilian olives
	salt and freshly ground pepper, to taste
1 tbsp	chopped fresh oregano
1 tbsp	chopped fresh parsley
1 can (14 oz)	artichoke hearts, drained and quartered

1 Preheat the oven to 350°F. Toss the chicken strips with the flour until coated. In an oven-proof Dutch oven, heat the oil and cook the onion and garlic and sauté until tender. Add the chicken strips and brown on all sides.

2 Add the chicken broth and the tomatoes and the olives and season to taste with salt and pepper. Bring to a boil. Cover, transfer to the oven and bake for 20 to 30 minutes.

3 Add the artichoke hearts and the fresh herbs and bake for 10 minutes longer. Taste for seasoning.

4 Serve piping hot over cooked egg noodles.

Oven-Roasted

Chicken Tenders
with Celery Remoulade

2 SERVINGS

⅔ cup	mayonnaise
¼ cup	plain yogurt
2 tbsp	chopped fresh parsley
2 tsp	Dijon mustard
	salt and freshly ground pepper, to taste
1	fresh celery root, peeled, shredded and blanched or 2 cups finely shredded cabbage
8	chicken tenders
	diced red and yellow pepper (garnish)

1 In a medium bowl, mix together the mayonnaise, yogurt, parsley, Dijon mustard and salt and pepper to taste.

2 Add the shredded celery root or cabbage and mix well. Cover and refrigerate for 3 to 6 hours before serving, if time allows.

3 Preheat the oven to 400°F. Place the chicken tenders on a greased baking sheet and season with salt and pepper. Cook for 10 minutes, turning the tenders halfway through cooking, until cooked through.

4 Arrange the chicken tenders on plates, accompanied with the celery remoulade, and garnish with the diced peppers.

Note

Celery root is a wonderful vegetable to experiment with, and can be eaten raw or cooked. On the outside, it resembles a large gnarled turnip, and its flavor is more pronounced than that of celery.

The tender is a very tender part of the chicken that is attached to the breast.

Oven-Roasted

Cheese-stuffed Chicken Breasts

4 SERVINGS

4	chicken breasts, skin removed
½ cup	gruyère cheese, grated
¼ cup	hazelnuts (or walnuts), chopped
½ cup	chopped blanched fresh spinach
¼ cup	all-purpose flour
2	eggs, lightly beaten
	pinch of ground nutmeg
	salt and freshly ground pepper, to taste
¼ cup	plain dry bread crumbs
2 tbsp	butter

1 Preheat the oven to 350°F. With a sharp knife, cut open a pocket lengthwise in the chicken breasts.

2 In a medium bowl, mix together the gruyère cheese, the spinach and hazelnuts. Spread this mixture evenly into the chicken breast pockets, pressing them closed. Dust the chicken with flour.

3 In a medium bowl, beat the eggs with the nutmeg and salt and pepper to taste. Dip the breasts into the egg mixture, and roll in the bread crumbs to cover.

4 In a large ovenproof nonstick skillet, melt the butter over medium heat. Cook the breasts for 2 minutes on each side. Transfer to the oven and bake for 15 to 20 minutes until cooked through.

Note
When serving, you can slice the breasts diagonally and accompany with a tomato sauce or salsa.

Oven-Roasted

Chicken Liver Flan

4 SERVINGS

1 cup	evaporated milk
½ lb	chicken livers, trimmed
3	eggs
1	egg yolk
	pinch of ground nutmeg
	salt and freshly ground pepper, to taste
	butter

1 Preheat the oven to 350°F. In a small saucepan, slowly heat the milk until almost boiling. Remove from the heat and set aside.

2 Using a food processor, purée the chicken livers with the eggs, egg yolk and nutmeg; season with salt and pepper. With the food processor running, add the hot milk and process until smooth. Press the mixture through a sieve into a bowl.

3 Transfer to 4 individual buttered 4- to 6-ounce custard cups. Place the cups in a baking pan and pour water into the pan to a depth of 1 in. Bake for 35 to 40 minutes.

4 Let sit for 10 minutes, then turn out onto serving plates. Serve the chicken liver flans as a first course, accompanied with a fresh tomato sauce or vegetable crudités and toasts.

Chicken Fondant

4 SERVINGS

2 tbsp	butter
4	skinless, boneless chicken breast halves
2 cups	tomato juice
1 tbsp	tomato paste
	pinch of sugar
1 tbsp	cornstarch, mixed with 2 tbsp of cold water
1 tbsp	chopped fresh parsley
	salt and freshly ground pepper, to taste

1 Preheat the oven to 350°F.

2 In a large ovenproof nonstick skillet, melt the butter over medium heat. Cook the chicken breasts for 2 minutes on each side. Transfer to the oven and bake for 15 to 20 minutes, until cooked through.

3 Meanwhile, in a medium non-aluminum saucepan, bring the tomato juice, tomato paste and sugar to a boil over medium heat. Season to taste with salt and pepper. Stir in the cornstarch mixture and cook, stirring, until thickened. Remove from the heat.

4 Coat 4 dinner plates or 1 serving platter with the sauce, and arrange the chicken breasts on top. Sprinkle with parsley and serve.

Note

For more variety, a hint of basil or orange zest can be added to this sauce. Or, if you like, bake the chicken with a sprinkling of parmesan cheese.

Oven-Roasted

Breaded Chicken

4 SERVINGS

½ cup	plain dry or Italian-seasoned bread crumbs
¼ cup	all-purpose flour
	salt and freshly ground pepper, to taste
8	bone-in chicken pieces, skin removed (legs, breasts and drumsticks)
3 tbsp	olive oil

1 Preheat the oven to 400°F.

2 In a pie plate, mix together the bread crumbs, flour and salt and pepper to taste.

3 Coat each piece of chicken in the flour-bread crumb mixture.

4 Heat the olive oil in a large, ovenproof non-stick skillet over medium-high heat. Add the chicken pieces and cook for 3 to 4 minutes, turning once, until browned. Transfer to the oven for 20 to 30 minutes, or until cooked through. Serve.

Oven-Roasted

Chicken Breasts
with Carrot Coulis

4 SERVINGS

1 cup	orange juice
2 tbsp	maple syrup or brown sugar
1 tbsp	finely chopped shallots
1 tbsp	vegetable oil
1 tsp	soy sauce
1 tsp	Dijon mustard
½ tsp	chopped garlic
½ tsp	dried oregano
½ tsp	dried savory
	salt and freshly ground pepper, to taste
4	large skinless, boneless chicken breast halves
¼ cup	all-purpose flour
2	eggs, beaten
1 cup	plain dry bread crumbs
2 tbsp	vegetable oil

Carrot Coulis

1 tbsp	butter
1 tbsp	chopped shallots
1	bay leaf
1	sprig of thyme
1	sprig of parsley
1 cup	chicken broth
1 cup	thinly sliced carrots,
¼ cup	dry white wine
	salt and freshly ground pepper, to taste
1 tsp	cornstarch, mixed with 1 tbsp cold water
¼ cup	light cream

1 In a large bowl, mix together the orange juice, maple syrup, shallots, oil, soy sauce, mustard, garlic and herbs; season to taste with salt and pepper. Add the chicken breasts and turn to coat. Cover and marinate in the refrigerator for 1 to 2 hours.

2 Preheat the oven to 350°F. Drain the marinade from the chicken, coat the chicken breasts in the flour, dip in the beaten egg, then dredge in the bread crumb, pressing them in firmly.

3 In a large nonstick, ovenproof skillet , heat the oil over the medium heat. Cook the chicken breasts for 2 minutes on each side, until golden. Transfer to the oven and bake for 10 to 12 minutes, until cooked through.

4 Meanwhile, in a medium saucepan, melt the butter over medium heat; sauté the shallots. Add herbs, broth, carrots and wine; bring to a boil. Season. Lower the heat, cover and simmer 15 minutes, until the carrots are tender. Add the cornstarch mixture; cook, stirring until thickened. Discard the herbs. Purée in a food processor. Add the cream. Serve with the chicken.

Oven-Roasted

Crispy Chicken Breasts
Parmentier

4 SERVINGS

3 tbsp	Dijon mustard
2	garlic cloves, finely chopped
	juice of ½ lemon
4	bone-in chicken breast halves, skin removed
1½ cups	peeled and grated potatoes
1½ tsp	olive oil
	salt and freshly ground pepper, to taste
	chopped chives or green onions, to taste

1 Preheat the oven to 425°F. In a cup, combine the mustard, garlic and lemon juice, and brush this mixture on the meat. Place the chicken in an oiled metal baking pan.

2 In a medium bowl, mix together the potatoes and olive oil. Cover each chicken breast with the potatoes; season to taste with salt and pepper.

3 Bake the chicken for 30 minutes, until the potatoes are golden and the chicken is no longer pink inside.

4 Broil the chicken for 2–3 minutes to brown the potatoes. Garnish with the chopped chives or green onions and serve immediately.

Note

If you prepare your potatoes in advance, keep them in a bowl of ice water, and drain and dry on a clean towel before using.

Oven-Roasted

Chef-style Chicken Breasts

4 SERVINGS

4	skinless, boneless chicken breast halves **(4 oz each)**
2 tbsp	grainy mustard
4	slices of cooked ham
4	gruyère or Swiss cheese slices
1 tbsp	butter
	salt and freshly ground pepper to taste
3	shallots, finely chopped
½ cup	chicken broth
1 tbsp	finely chopped fresh cilantro
1 tbsp	cornstarch, mixed with 2 tbsp cold water

1 Preheat the oven to 350°F. With a sharp knife, cut the breasts in half lengthwise, leaving an edge attached to form a pocket (like a wallet). Gently flatten the breasts. Coat the inside with the mustard, and place 1 slice of ham and another of cheese inside each. Roll them up and secure with toothpicks.

2 In a large nonstick skillet, melt the butter over medium heat and brown the chicken. Season with salt and pepper. Transfer to a pie plate and bake for 20 to 25 minutes, until cooked through.

3 In the same skillet, cook the shallots over medium heat. Add the chicken broth and cilantro, and simmer for 5 minutes. Add the cornstarch mixture and cook, stirring, until thickened.

4 Remove the toothpicks from the chicken and slice the rolls, if you like. Arrange on a serving plate and serve with the sauce in a sauceboat.

Oven-Roasted

Honey and Mustard Chicken

4 SERVINGS

4	skinless, boneless chicken breast halves
3 tbsp	all-purpose flour
1 tbsp	vegetable oil
1 tbsp	butter
¼ cup	dry white wine
2 tbsp	honey
2 tbsp	Dijon mustard
	pinch of dried oregano
	or
1 tbsp	chopped fresh oregano
	salt and freshly ground pepper, to taste

1 Preheat the oven to 350°F. Lightly flour the chicken. In a large nonstick skillet, heat the oil and butter over medium-high heat. Add the chicken and cook, turning once, until browned for 5 minutes.

2 Transfer to the oven and bake for 10 minutes, or until cooked through.

3 Transfer chicken to a platter; cover to keep warm. Discard any excess fat from the skillet, deglaze with the wine and cook over medium heat until reduced by half. Add the honey, mustard and oregano, and season with salt and pepper. Stir well and bring to a boil.

4 Add the chicken and turn to coat well with the sauce. Serve.

Oven-Roasted

Lemon and Soy Chicken

4 SERVINGS

2	lemon tea bags
2 cups	boiling water
2	lemons
6	bread slices
⅓ cup	milk
8	skinless, boneless chicken thighs
1 tbsp	butter
½ cup	sugar
2 tbsp	white wine vinegar
2 tbsp	soy sauce

1 Preheat the oven to 400°F. Steep the tea bags in the water. Grate the zest of the 2 lemons. Peel the white pith from the lemons and cut the lemons in pieces.

2 Soak the bread slices in the milk with the lemon zest; season with salt and pepper and mix well with a fork. Stuff the chicken thighs with the bread mixture and seal to form a bundle. Fasten with toothpicks.

3 Melt the butter in a large skillet over medium heat. Add the thighs and brown. Arrange in a 13 x 9 in. baking dish. Return the skillet to the heat. Add the sugar and vinegar. Stir and cook until light amber. Carefully add the tea, the lemon pieces and the soy sauce. Bring to a boil.

4 Pour the lemon/tea mixture over the chicken, and bake for 40 minutes, until cooked through. Remove the thighs and keep warm. Reduce the sauce in a saucepan over medium heat for 5 minutes, strain and serve with the chicken.

Note
Serve with white and wild rice mix.

Oven-Roasted

Chicken Pizza

4 SERVINGS

2 tbsp	olive oil
1 lb	ground chicken
1 tsp	ground cumin
½ tsp	dried oregano
1	garlic clove, minced
	salt and freshly ground pepper, to taste
4	8-in. flour tortillas
¾ cup	prepared cheese salsa
1½ cups	grated Monterey Jack or pepper jack cheese
1	large tomato, diced
5	green onions, thinly sliced
½ cup	chopped pitted green olives
½ cup	chopped pitted black olives
2 to 4 tbsp	chopped pickled jalapeno pepper

1 In a large nonstick skillet, heat the oil over medium-high heat. Add the the ground chicken, cumin, oregano and garlic, and season to taste with salt and pepper. Cook and stir until the chicken loses its pink color; remove from the heat.

2 Preheat the broiler. On a large cookie sheet, place 2 tortillas side by side and crisp each side under the broiler. Repeat with the other 2 tortillas. Turn the oven to 400°F.

3 Spread the cheese salsa over 2 of the tortillas on the cookie sheet and top with the other 2 tortillas. Spoon the chicken mixture over and sprinkle with the cheese. Sprinkle with the tomato, green onions, green and black olives and jalapeno pepper.

4 Bake for 8 to 12 minutes or until the cheese has melted. Cut into wedges and serve.

Crispy Chicken Casserole

4 SERVINGS

1	packet of onion soup mix
1½ cups	buttermilk
1 tbsp	all-purpose flour
2	garlic cloves, finely chopped
	freshly ground pepper, to taste
4	skinless, boneless chicken breast halves
2 cups	frozen mixed vegetables
¼ cup	plain dry bread crumbs
1 tbsp	butter, cut up
	paprika, to taste

1 Preheat the oven to 350°F. In a medium bowl, combine the onion soup mix, buttermilk, flour, garlic and pepper. Mix well.

2 Place the chicken breasts in a lightly greased 11 x 17 in. baking dish and add the soup mixture.

3 Cover with foil and bake for 20 minutes. Remove the cover and add the vegetables.

4 Sprinkle with the bread crumbs and dot with the butter. Bake, uncovered, approximately 25 minutes longer, until the chicken is cooked through. Sprinkle with paprika before serving.

Note

When serving, a few drops of fresh lemon will heighten the flavor.

Can't find any buttermilk? Make it yourself by mixing 1 cup of milk with 2 tsp of white vinegar. Shake and let stand for several minutes, and voilà, there you have it!

Oven-Roasted

Chicken Soufflé

4 SERVINGS

1 cup	dry bread crusts
½ cup	milk
1 tbsp	olive oil
1 cup	thinly sliced mushrooms
1	celery stalk, finely chopped
½	onion, finely chopped
3	egg yolks
½	red pepper, cut in small cubes
3 cups	chopped cooked white meat of chicken
	salt and freshly ground pepper, to taste
½ tsp	paprika
3	egg whites

1 Preheat the oven to 325°F. In a medium bowl, soak the bread crusts in the milk and let sit for 5 minutes.

2 Meanwhile, heat the olive oil in a medium nonstick skillet over medium heat. Add the mushrooms, onion and celery and cook, stirring often for 5 minutes; set aside.

3 In a large bowl, mix together the chicken, egg yolks, red pepper, the onion-celery-mushroom mixture, and the bread crusts. Season with salt, pepper and paprika; set aside.

4 Beat the egg whites until stiff with an electric mixer, at high speed. Gently fold into the chicken mixture. Transfer to a 1- to 1½-quart buttered soufflé dish and bake for 50 to 60 minutes, or until a knife inserted in the center comes out clean. Serve immediately.

Oven-Roasted

Large Stuffed Canapés

24 CANAPÉS

2 or 3	large skinless, boneless chicken breast halves, cooked and cooled
½ can (5 oz)	condensed cream of mushroom soup
1	egg
1	small onion, chopped
2	celery stalks, finely diced
2 tbsp	chopped fresh parsley
	salt and freshly ground pepper, to taste
4	sesame seed hamburger buns

1 Preheat the oven to 375°F.

2 In a food processor, finely chop the chicken breasts. Add the cream of mushroom soup and the egg and pulse to mix. Add the celery, onion and parsley, and season with salt and pepper. Pulse to mix.

3 Hollow out each hamburger bun, making a shell and, using a spoon or pastry bag, stuff with the chicken mixture and close the buns.

4 Place the stuffed buns on a baking sheet and bake for 10 minutes, until heated through. Remove from the oven, cut each bun into six triangles and place on a serving platter. Serve with crudités.

Oven-Roasted

Chicken Casserole à la Carbonara

6 SERVINGS

1 tbsp	vegetable oil
1	small chicken, cut into 8 pieces
	salt and freshly ground pepper, to taste
½ lb	bacon
2	green onions, sliced
4 tbsp	butter
1 cup	heavy cream
	pinch of dried oregano
	pinch crushed red pepper
⅔ cup	grated parmesan
2 cups	hot, freshly cooked spaghetti
3	eggs, beaten

1 Preheat the oven to 350°F. In a large, deep ovenproof skillet, heat the oil over medium heat. Add the chicken and cook until browned. Season to taste with salt and pepper and bake for approximately 35 minutes, until cooked through.

2 Meanwhile in a large skillet, cook the bacon over medium heat until very crispy, and add the green onions. Discard any excess fat.

3 Lower the heat and stir in the butter, cream, oregano and crushed red pepper. Mix together and add ⅓ cup parmesan. Bring to a boil and let simmer for 1 or 2 minutes. Add the spaghetti.

4 Add the eggs and toss until the spaghetti is coated and heated through. Remove from the heat. Place the spaghetti on a serving platter. Top with the chicken pieces and sprinkle with the remaining parmesan cheese and serve.

Note

For a less rich version of this delicious dish, replace the cream with crushed tomatoes in mixed herbs. And why not add a little garlic if you like your dishes highly seasoned—it's delicious!

Oven-Roasted

Chicken with Rum and Pineapple

4 to 6 SERVINGS

4 tbsp	butter
2	onions, chopped
1 cup	dark rum
	juice of 1 lime
1	fresh pineapple, peeled, cored and cut in chunks
	salt and freshly ground pepper, to taste
1	whole chicken

1 Preheat the oven to 375°F.

2 In a heavy Dutch oven, melt the butter over medium heat. Add the onions, and cook, stirring often, until tender. Deglaze with the rum and the lime juice, bring to a boil and simmer until reduced by a third.

3 Stir in the pineapple chunks and season to taste with salt and pepper. Place the chicken on top of the pineapple and season the chicken. Cover and bake, for 1 hour.

4 Remove the cover, baste with the pan juices and bake uncovered, for 20 to 30 minutes longer, until the chicken is golden and cooked through.

Note
For a smoother sauce, thicken with a bit of cornstarch.

Oven-Roasted

Tarragon Chicken

6 SERVINGS

4½ lb	large chicken
	salt and freshly ground pepper, to taste
½ cup	chopped fresh tarragon
1 tbsp	butter
4	shallots, chopped
2	garlic cloves, chopped
¾ cup	dry white wine
1 cup	chicken broth
	juice of 1 orange

1 Preheat the oven to 425°F. Salt and pepper the chicken inside and outside and place on a rack in a roasting pan. Place half of the tarragon inside. Roast the chicken for 15 to 20 minutes, until browned.

2 Meanwhile, in a heavy medium saucepan, melt the butter over medium heat. Add the shallots and garlic and cook, stirring, until tender.

3 Deglaze with the white wine and add the broth. Bring to a boil and let simmer for 5 minutes. Add the orange juice. Pour over the chicken, cover loosely with foil. Lower the oven to 350°F and roast for approximately 1 hour, until cooked through.

4 Place the chicken on a platter. Skim any fat from the pan juices and stir in the remaining tarragon. Taste for seasoning and serve the sauce with the chicken.

Oven-Roasted

Maple Chicken

4 SERVINGS

4	skinless, boneless chicken breast halves
1 tbsp	vegetable oil
1 tbsp	butter
2	shallots, chopped
¼ cup	dry white wine
⅓ cup	chicken broth
¼ to ⅓ cup	pure maple syrup
	salt and freshly ground pepper, to taste

1 Preheat the oven to 350°F. In a large nonstick skillet, heat the oil and butter over medium-high heat. Add the chicken and cook, turning once, for 5 minutes.

2 Transfer to an ovenproof dish and bake for approximately 10 minutes, or until cooked through. Transfer to a serving platter. Cover to keep warm.

3 Meanwhile, in the same skillet over medium heat, cook the shallots until tender. Deglaze with the broth and white wine, and let reduce by half. Add the maple syrup and season to taste with salt and pepper.

4 Cook over medium heat until the sauce begins to boil. Spoon over the chicken and serve.

Oven-Roasted

Marinated Chicken Drumsticks
with Rosemary

4 SERVINGS

¼ cup	dry red wine
2 tbsp	olive oil or vegetable oil
2 tsp	grated lemon zest
2	garlic cloves, finely chopped
1 tsp	dried rosemary or
1 tbsp	fresh rosemary
8	chicken drumsticks
	salt and freshly ground pepper, to taste
	sprigs of fresh rosemary or chives (garnish)

1 In a large glass bowl, combine the red wine, oil, lemon zest, garlic and rosemary, and mix well. Add the chicken drumsticks and coat well with the marinade.

2 Cover and marinate in the refrigerator for 1½ to 2 hours, turning frequently. Drain off the marinade.

3 Preheat the broiler. Arrange the drumsticks on a broiler-pan rack and broil 6 in. from the heat for 5 or 6 minutes on each side. Turn the oven to 350°F. Bake the drumsticks for 30 minutes, or until cooked through.

4 Season to taste with salt and pepper; garnish with sprigs of rosemary or chives and serve.

Note
Instead of broiling, the drumsticks can be browned in a lightly oiled skillet over medium heat for 5 minutes on each side before placing in the oven to finish cooking.

Oven-Roasted

Express Chicken Wings

4 SERVINGS

24	chicken wings
2 tbsp	butter
1	onion, finely chopped
1	garlic clove, minced
1 tsp	paprika
½ tsp	ground cumin
1 cup	hot chicken broth
1 tbsp	cornstarch, mixed with 2 tbsp cold water

1 Cut off the bonier small tip of the wings and keep for other uses. Grasp the tip of the wing and push the meat downwards with a small knife, following the bone, to form a small ball around the bone joint.

2 Melt the butter in a measuring cup in a microwave oven on high (100%) for 1 minute. Add the onion, garlic, paprika and cumin, and microwave on high (100%) for another 1½ minutes, until the onion is tender.

3 Dip each wing in the melted butter and place in a circle in a Pyrex dish. Cover with vented plastic wrap, and microwave on medium-high (80%) for 8 minutes.

4 Spoon over the chicken broth. Microwave on medium (60%) for 3 minutes, until cooked through. Pour the pan juices into a saucepan. Stir in the cornstarch mixture and cook over medium heat, stirring until thickened. Serve with the wings.

Oven-Roasted

Stuffed Chicken Rolls

4 SERVINGS

4	large skinless, boneless chicken breast halves
	salt and freshly ground pepper, to taste
4	thin slices of cooked ham
4	thin slices of Swiss cheese
12	fresh thin asparagus spears, cooked crisp-tender
2 tbsp	all-purpose flour
1 tbsp	butter
1 tbsp	vegetable oil
1 cup	home-made or prepared marinara sauce, heated
2 tbsp	chopped fresh parsley
4	lemon quarters

1 Preheat the oven to 350°F. Cover the chicken breasts with waxed paper and gently flatten to ¼-in thickness with a rolling pin.

2 Season to taste with salt and pepper. Place one slice of ham, a slice of cheese and three asparagus spears on each of the breasts. Roll up carefully and secure with toothpicks. Sprinkle with flour.

3 In a large, ovenproof nonstick skillet, heat the butter and the oil over medium heat. Add the chicken and cook, turning once, until browned. Transfer to the oven and bake for 12 to 15 minutes, until cooked through. Arrange on a serving plate.

4 Serve hot, accompanied with marinara sauce, lemon quarters and parsley.

Note
A variation: you can dredge the chicken rolls in flour, a beaten egg, and bread crumbs before browning.

Oven-Roasted

Chicken Émincé

2 SERVINGS

Chicken

2 tbsp	butter
2	skinless, boneless chicken breast halves, sliced thinly
2 tbsp	chicken broth
	clove of garlic, thinly sliced
½ tsp	paprika
½ tsp	dried tarragon
	freshly ground pepper, to taste

Garnish

3	green onions, sliced
½	red pepper, cubed
½	green pepper, cubed
2 cups	cooked rice
1 tbsp	soy sauce
2 tbsp	sesame seeds

1 Melt 1 tbsp butter in a large nonstick skillet over medium-high heat. Add the chicken and cook, tossing often, until lightly browned.

2 Add the chicken broth, garlic, paprika, tarragon and season with salt and pepper. Cook, stirring often, for 3 to 4 minutes, until chicken is cooked through. Set aside and keep warm in a dish.

3 In the same skillet, melt the remaining 1 tbsp butter. Add the green onions and peppers and cook, stirring often, until lightly browned and tender.

4 Add the rice, sesame seeds and soy sauce and heat through. Serve the chicken on a bed of rice.

Sautéed

Peanut Chicken

4 SERVINGS

Chicken

1 lb	skinless, boneless chicken breast, cubed
1 tbsp	cornstarch
1 tbsp	thinly sliced fresh ginger
2	garlic cloves, thinly sliced
1 to 2 tsp	crushed red pepper
3 tbsp	vegetable oil
½ cup	unsalted peanuts
1 cup	sliced green pepper

Sauce

¼ cup	rice wine vinegar
2 tbsp	honey
1 tbsp	soy sauce
2 tbsp	chicken broth
2 tbsp	smooth peanut butter

1 In a medium bowl, mix together the chicken, cornstarch, ginger, garlic and the crushed red pepper; set aside.

2 In a large heavy skillet or a wok, heat the oil over medium-high heat; add the peanuts and sauté for 1 minute, or until the peanuts are golden. Remove from the pan and set aside.

3 Add the chicken to the skillet or wok. Stir-fry for 2 to 3 minutes, or until the chicken is no longer pink. Add the green pepper and stir-fry for another 1 or 2 minutes, until tender.

4 Combine all the sauce ingredients in a small bowl, mixing until smooth. Add to the skillet or wok, and bring to a boil, stirring constantly. Let boil 1 minute to thicken, and add the peanuts. Serve.

Sautéed

Spicy Szechuan Chicken Wings

4 to 6 SERVINGS

2 to 2½ lb chicken wings

2 tbsp cornstarch

1/4 cup vegetable oil

1/3 cup corn syrup

1/4 cup soy sauce

1 tsp thinly sliced fresh ginger

1 garlic clove, thinly sliced

1 to 2 tsp crushed red pepper

diagonally sliced scallions (garnish)

 **1** Remove the wing tips; cut the wings in two at the joint.

2 In a large bowl, mix the chicken wings with the cornstarch.

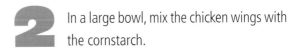 **3** In a large, heavy, deep skillet or wok, heat the vegetable oil over medium-high heat until hot but not smoking. Add the chicken wings and sauté until they are cooked and golden on both sides; approximately 10 to 15 minutes. Drain off any excess fat from the pan.

4 Combine the corn syrup, soy sauce, ginger, garlic and crushed red pepper; add to the skillet or wok and continue to sauté until the wings are well coated. Serve immediately, garnished with sliced scallions.

Sautéed

Chicken Biryani

2 SERVINGS

Rice

1 tbsp	butter
1¾ cups	boiling salted water
1 cup	basmati rice, rinsed
½ tsp	garam masala*
¼ cup	raisins
1 tsp	chopped fresh ginger

Chicken

2 tbsp	vegetable oil
½ tsp	garam masala
½ tsp	ground turmeric
½ tsp	ground coriander
½ tsp	ground cumin
1 lb	chicken drumsticks and/or thighs
1	medium onion, finely chopped
	salt and freshly ground pepper, to taste

*Garam masala

10	cardamom seeds
1 tbsp	whole black peppercorns
2 tsp	cumin seeds
½ tsp	coriander seeds
2	small dried red peppers, seeds removed
2	pinches of ground cinnamon

Crush all ingredients to a powder in a clean coffee grinder or a food processor.

Garam masala can be kept in a sealed container for up to 3 months.

Note

For garnish, you may add some toasted sliced almonds and decorate the edges of the plate, with tomato slices and hard-boiled egg wedges.

1 Preheat the oven to 350°F. In a medium saucepan over high heat, melt the butter in the boiling salted water. Add the rice and garam masala, lower the heat, cover and cook, until the water is almost evaporated, about 10 minutes. Set aside.

2 Meanwhile, heat the oil in a large heavy skillet over medium heat. Add the spices, chicken and onion. Cook, stirring often, until browned. Season to taste with salt and pepper.

3 Spoon out the rice into a large baking dish and add the raisins and ginger. Place the chicken and pan juices on top, cover with foil and bake for ½ hour, to allow the rice to soften and finish cooking the chicken.

4 Serve the chicken and rice from the baking dish or arrrange on a large platter.

Sautéed

Émincé Bangkok Style

4 SERVINGS

½ lb	beef filet mignon
½ lb	skinless, boneless chicken breast
½ lb	medium shrimp, shelled and deveined
1	garlic clove, chopped
3 tbsp	vegetable oil
½ cup	dry white wine
½ cup	sugar
1¼ cups	chicken broth
1 tsp	Tabasco sauce
2 tsp	cornstarch mixed with 1 tbsp cold water
⅔ cup	bean sprouts (optional)
1 cup	stemmed sliced fresh shiitake mushrooms
⅓ cup	cashews
⅓ cup	pine nuts

1 Slice the filet mignon, chicken and shrimp into strips, and set aside in the refrigerator.

2 In a heavy medium saucepan, sauté the garlic in 1 tbsp oil over medium heat. Add the white wine and sugar, and bring to a boil, stirring to dissolve the sugar. Simmer until reduced by half. Add the chicken broth and the Tabasco sauce, and let simmer for 5 minutes.

3 Stir in the cornstarch mixture and bring to a boil, stirring. Let simmer for another 5 minutes. Set aside.

4 In a large heavy skillet, heat the remaining 2 tbsp oil over high heat. Add the chicken and the filet mignon and cook, turning often, until brown. Add the shrimp, bean sprouts if using, and the mushrooms and stir-fry until the shrimp and the chicken are cooked through. Add the sauce and the pine nuts and cashews and heat through. Serve immediately.

Sautéed

Szechuan Chicken
with Chinese Vermicelli

4 SERVINGS

1¼ lb	skinless, boneless chicken breast
2 tbsp	cornstarch
2	egg whites, lightly beaten
1 tsp	baking powder
3 tbsp	peanut oil
1	red pepper, cubed
2	green onions, chopped
1 tbsp	chopped fresh garlic
1 tbsp	sesame seeds
2 tbsp	soy sauce
2 tbsp	rice wine
1 tbsp	light corn syrup
¾ lb	Chinese vermicelli, cooked
2 tbsp	chopped fresh cilantro or fresh parsley
1	green onion, sliced thinly

1 Cut the chicken breast into thin strips. Place in a large bowl and set aside.

2 In a small bowl, mix together the cornstarch, egg whites and baking powder. Pour over the chicken; mix well.

3 In a large heavy skillet or wok, heat the oil over medium-high heat. Add the chicken and stir-fry until golden. Add the pepper, green onions, garlic and sesame seeds. Stir-fry for several minutes, until the chicken is cooked through and the vegetables tender.

4 Add the soy sauce, rice wine, corn syrup and the Chinese vermicelli; mix well and heat slowly. Garnish with cilantro or parsley and the green onion, and serve.

Sautéed

Sautéed Chicken with Apricots

4 SERVINGS

8	fresh or dried apricots* see note, rinsed
2 tbsp	olive oil
1 tbsp	butter
1 lb	skinless, boneless chicken breast, cubed
1	onion, chopped
¼ cup	chicken broth
	salt and freshly ground pepper, to taste
1 tbsp	fresh thyme (garnish)

1 If using fresh apricots, cut them in half, remove the pit and cut into chunks. If using dried apricots, cut into small pieces.

2 In a large nonstick skillet, heat the oil and melt the butter over medium-high heat. Add the chicken and onion and cook, stirring often, until browned.

3 Add the apricots and continue cooking for several minutes, until the chicken is cooked through. Deglaze with the chicken broth, and season to taste with salt and pepper.

4 Arrange the chicken, apricots and pan juices on a warmed plate. Sprinkle with the thyme. Serve immediately, with rice or mashed potatoes as a side dish.

Note
If you use dried apricots, they must be steeped in warm water for 20 minutes before use.

Sautéed

Chicken Satay

4 SERVINGS

3 tbsp	vegetable oil
2 tbsp	peeled and finely chopped fresh ginger
4	garlic cloves, finely chopped
1¼ lb	skinless, boneless chicken breast, cut in long strips
2 tsp	chili powder
¼ cup	smooth peanut butter
6	green onions, thinly sliced
1 cup	canned unsweetened coconut milk
2 tbsp	honey
	salt and freshly ground pepper, to taste
2 tbsp	chopped fresh cilantro
¼ cup	chopped peanuts

1 Heat the oil in a large heavy skillet or a wok over high heat until hot but not smoking. Add the ginger and garlic and cook, stirring, until fragrant.

2 Add the chicken and stir-fry for 3 to 4 minutes, until golden.

3 Lower the heat and stir in the peanut butter, green onions and chili powder. Gradually add the coconut milk and honey, stirring until the sauce is creamy and bubbly. Season to taste with salt and pepper; let simmer for 5 minutes.

4 Arrange the chicken on serving plates, coat with the sauce and garnish with cilantro and chopped peanuts. Serve with rice, sautéed vegetables and jasmine tea.

Sautéed

Thai Green Curry Chicken

4 SERVINGS

1 tbsp	vegetable oil
1	onion, thinly sliced
2	garlic cloves, chopped
2 tsp	green curry paste
1 lb	skinless, boneless chicken breast and thighs, cut in chunks
1 cup	julienne-cut snow peas
1	red pepper, thinly sliced
1½ cups	canned unsweetened coconut milk
1 tbsp	fish sauce
	grated zest and juice of 1 lime
	sugar, to taste
¼ cup	fresh cilantro leaves

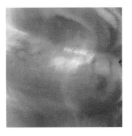

1 In a wok or a large, heavy, deep skillet, heat the oil over medium-high heat. Sauté the onion and garlic until tender. Stir in the green curry paste and cook, stirring, for 1 minute.

2 Add the chicken, stirring well to coat each piece with the curry. Cook, stirring often, for 2 to 3 minutes. Add the vegetables and sauté for another minute.

3 Add the coconut milk and bring to a boil. Add the fish sauce, lime zest and juice, and sugar to taste. Lower the heat and let simmer for several minutes, until the chicken is cooked through.

4 Arrange on a serving dish and sprinkle with cilantro. Serve with sticky rice or jasmine rice.

Sautéed

Chicken in Red Curry

2 SERVINGS

1 tbsp	vegetable oil
1 tbsp	red curry paste
2	skinless, boneless chicken breast halves, cut in chunks
⅔ cup	canned unsweetened coconut milk
1 cup	frozen cut green beans
	salt, to taste
½ tsp	sugar
4 to 5	basil leaves (garnish)
½	red pepper, cut into small pieces (garnish)
½	green pepper, cut into small pieces (garnish)

1 Stir together the oil and the curry paste in a large heavy skillet over medium-high heat. Add the chicken pieces, and sauté for several minutes until coated with the curry mixture.

2 Stir in the coconut milk and the green beans. Lower the heat and continue cooking until the chicken is cooked through, approximately 10 minutes.

3 Add salt to taste and the sugar.

4 Arrange on a serving platter; garnish with the basil leaves and peppers.

Sautéed

Yin-Yang of Chicken
and Cashew Nuts

4 SERVINGS

¼ **cup**	light corn syrup
3 tbsp	soy sauce
1 tbsp	grated fresh ginger
2	garlic cloves, finely chopped
1 tsp	sesame oil toasted
½ **tsp**	crushed red pepper flakes
¾ **lb**	skinless, boneless chicken breast, cut in thin strips
2 tbsp	vegetable oil
½ **cup**	unsalted cashews
1½ cups	broccoli florets
½	medium onion, sliced thinly
½	red pepper, cut into fine strips
½ **cup**	water
1 can (15 oz)	baby corn, drained
1½ cups	diagonally cut snow peas
1 cup	bean sprouts (optional)
2 tbsp	cornstarch
2 tsp	chicken broth granules

1 In a medium bowl, mix together the corn syrup, soy sauce, ginger, garlic, sesame oil and the crushed red pepper flakes. Add the chicken and mix well. Cover and marinate for 30 minutes. Drain the chicken and reserve the marinade.

2 In a large heavy skillet or wok, heat the vegetable oil over medium heat. Sauté the cashews for 1 minute or until they are golden. Remove and set aside.

3 Stir-fry the chicken in the skillet for 2 to 3 minutes, until the pink color is gone. Add the broccoli, onion and pepper, and stir-fry for 1 or 2 minutes. Add the water, baby corn, snow peas and bean sprouts, if using, cover and cook for 3 to 4 minutes, or until the vegetables are tender yet still crunchy.

4 Mix the cornstarch with the broth granules and the reserved marinade, and add to the chicken in the skillet. Let simmer, stirring, for 5 minutes, until thickened. Transfer to a serving plate, garnish with the cashews and serve.

Sautéed

Chicken Émincé
with Vegetables

2 SERVINGS

1 cup	Chinese rice noodles or cellophane noodles
	cold water
2 tsp	toasted sesame oil
2	green onions, chopped
1	garlic clove, minced
1 tsp	finely chopped fresh ginger
½ lb	skinless, boneless chicken breast, cut in chunks
½	red pepper, thinly sliced
1	carrot, thinly sliced diagonally
1 cup	broccoli florets
1 cup	cauliflower florets
1½ cups	chicken broth
½ cup	diagonally cut snow peas

Sauce

2 tbsp	cornstarch
2 tbsp	soy sauce
2 tbsp	hoisin sauce (optional)
2 tsp	toasted sesame oil
¼ tsp	Chinese chili paste or Tabasco sauce

1 Place the Chinese rice noodles or cellophane noodles in a large bowl, cover with cold water and let soften for 5 to 8 minutes. Drain well and set aside.

2 In a wok or a large nonstick skillet, heat the sesame oil over medium-high heat. Add the green onions, garlic and ginger and cook; stirring until wilted.

3 Add the chicken and stir-fry for 2 minutes. Add all the vegetables, except the snow peas. Add the chicken broth and bring to a boil. Lower the heat, cover and cook for 3 to 4 minutes, or until the vegetables are tender yet still crunchy.

4 Mix all sauce ingredients in a small bowl. Add the snow peas and the noodles to the wok or skillet. Stir in the sauce mixture and cook for 1 minute, stirring, until the sauce thickens. Serve in deep bowls.

Sautéed

Sweet and Sour Chicken Vegetable Sauté

4 SERVINGS

¾ cup	prepared sweet and sour sauce
2 tsp	finely chopped fresh ginger
2 drops	Tabasco sauce
1½ lb	skinless, boneless chicken breast, cubed
1 tbsp	cornstarch mixed with 1 tbsp cold water
1 cup	sliced carrots, blanched
1 cup	cauliflower florets, blanched
1 cup	broccoli florets, blanched
2	green onions, sliced (garnish)
2 tsp	snipped fresh rosemary (garnish)

1 Mix together the sweet and sour sauce, ginger, Tabasco sauce and the chicken in a microwave-safe dish or casserole.

2 Microwave uncovered on high (100%) for 6 to 9 minutes, stirring every 3 minutes, until the chicken is cooked through.

3 Stir in the cornstarch mixture and microwave for 1 minute. Stir well.

4 Add the vegetables to the chicken mixture and microwave on high for 3 to 5 minutes, or until heated through. Garnish with slices of green onion and rosemary. Serve immediately.

Sautéed

Chicken Liver with Mushrooms

6 SERVINGS

1½ lb	chicken livers, trimmed
¼ cup	all-purpose flour
	salt and freshly ground pepper, to taste
1 tbsp	vegetable oil
1 tbsp	butter
1	shallot, chopped
1	garlic clove, minced
1 cup	sliced white mushrooms
1 cup	thinly sliced oyster mushroom,
⅓ cup	chicken broth
2 tbsp	raspberry vinegar
¼ cup	heavy cream
2 tbsp	chopped fresh chives

1 Pat dry the chicken livers, cutting them in two if large. On a plate, mix together the flour and salt and pepper to taste. Dredge the chicken livers in the seasoned flour, shaking off any excess.

2 In a large heavy skillet, heat the oil and melt the butter over medium-high heat. Add the shallot and garlic and cook, stirring, until fragrant.

3 Add the livers and the mushrooms and cook, stirring often, for 4 to 5 minutes, until the livers are firm and pink inside. Transfer the livers to a heated platter.

4 Pour the broth and vinegar into the skillet and bring to a boil, stirring. Add the livers and the mushrooms. Stir in the cream and heat through. Taste for seasoning, sprinkle with the chopped chives and serve immediately.

Sautéed

Sautéed Chicken Liver

6 SERVINGS

1½ lb	chicken livers, trimmed
¼ cup	all-purpose flour
	salt and freshly ground pepper, to taste
1 tbsp	butter
1 tbsp	vegetable oil
1	garlic clove, minced
1 cup	drained, cooked frozen small pearl onions,
3 tbsp	water
2 tbsp	red wine vinegar
2 tbsp	red wine
2 tbsp	fresh thyme leaves (garnish)

1 Pat dry the chicken livers, cutting in two if large. In a plastic bag, mix together the flour and salt and pepper to taste. Place the chicken livers inside the bag and shake to coat well with the seasoned flour.

2 In a heavy large skillet, heat the oil and melt the butter over medium-high heat. Add the garlic and cook, stirring often, until fragrant.

3 Add the livers to the skillet and cook, stirring often, for 4 to 5 minutes, until the livers are firm and pink inside. Transfer the livers to a heated platter.

4 Add the vinegar and wine to the skillet and bring to a boil, stirring. Add the livers and pearl onions and toss to coat with the pan juices and heat through. Serve immediately, garnished with the thyme.

Sautéed

Chicken Casserole with Pearl Barley

4 SERVINGS

1 tbsp	butter
2½ lb	chicken cut into 8 pieces
	salt and freshly ground pepper, to taste
1 cup	cubed onions
½ cup	cubed celery
1½ cups	matchstick-cut peeled white turnip
1½ cups	matchstick-cut carrots
1 tsp	chopped fresh garlic
5 cups	chicken broth
1 cup	pearl barley
2 tbsp	chopped fresh parsley (garnish)

1 In a Dutch oven, melt the butter over medium-high heat. Add the chicken pieces and brown on all sides; season to taste with salt and pepper.

2 Add the onion and celery and continue cooking, stirring often, until tender.

3 Add the turnip, carrots, garlic and chicken broth. Bring to a boil, reduce the heat, cover and let simmer for 15 minutes. Add the barley, cover and let simmer approximately 30 minutes longer, until the barley is tender and the chicken cooked through.

4 Sprinkle with parsley and serve in deep soup plates.

Note

Skim the fat from the broth before adding the barley. Grains such as barley and wheat semolina are often overlooked ingredients in the kitchen; yet, they are very delicious and very good for you.

Simmered

Chicken Stew in a Loaf

4 SERVINGS

4	kaiser rolls (about 4 in. round)
1 cup	chicken broth
1 cup	milk
2 tbsp	butter
2	shallots, thinly sliced
2 tbsp	all-purpose flour
	salt and freshly ground pepper, to taste
2 tbsp	vegetable oil
1 lb	skinless, boneless chicken breast, cubed
2 cups	sliced mushrooms
2 tbsp	Madeira wine
2	carrots, cubed and blanched
1 cup	small cauliflower florets, blanched
1 cup	small broccoli florets, blanched

1 Preheat the oven to 350°F. Cut the tops off the rolls, and hollow out, leaving ½ in. thick walls. Place the rolls and their covers on a baking sheet and bake until they are browned, approximately 10 to 15 minutes.

2 In a small saucepan, bring the broth and milk to a boil. In a heavy medium saucepan, melt the butter over medium heat and sauté the shallots. Stir in the flour and cook, stirring, for 2 minutes. Add the hot liquid to the shallots while whisking. Lower the heat and let simmer for 20 minutes. Season to taste with salt and pepper.

3 In a large heavy saucepan, heat the oil over high heat. Add the chicken and mushrooms, and cook, stirring often, for 5 minutes or until golden. Add the Madeira and reduce by half. Add the sauce, lower the heat, cover and let simmer for 15 minutes.

4 Add the carrots, cauliflower and the broccoli, and warm through. Divide the chicken stew into the toasted rolls. Place the "cover" on the side and serve.

Simmered

Braised Chicken
with Aramé Seaweed

8 SERVINGS

2 tbsp	vegetable oil
3 lb	skinless, boneless chicken breast, cubed
2	medium onions, cubed
2	carrots, cut diagonally
¼ cup	dry white wine or rice vinegar
¾ cup	soy sauce
¼ cup	honey
2 cups	chicken broth
	salt and freshly ground pepper, to taste
⅓ cup	Aramé seaweed (optional)
1 tbsp	cornstarch mixed with 1 tbsp cold water

1 In a Dutch oven, heat the oil over high heat. Add the chicken cubes and onions and cook, stirring often, until golden.

2 Add the carrots, wine or the vinegar, soy sauce, honey and chicken broth and bring to a boil. Season to taste with salt and pepper, lower the heat, cover and let simmer for 30 minutes, until the chicken is very tender.

3 Stir in the Aramé, if using, and the cornstarch mixture and cook, stirring until thickened. Cover and let simmer for another 5 minutes.

4 Serve this meal in deep dishes, accompanied with steamed white rice.

Simmered

Chicken, Barley and Mushrooms
en Cocotte

4 SERVINGS

2 tbsp	vegetable oil
1½ lb	skinless, boneless chicken breast, cut in ½ in cubes
2	onions, thinly sliced
2 cups	quartered small mushrooms
2	green peppers, sliced thinly
1 can (28 oz)	diced tomatoes with juice
1⅓ cups	pearl barley
1½ cups	chicken broth
2 tsp	chopped fresh thyme
	salt and freshly ground pepper, to taste
2 tbsp	finely chopped fresh parsley

1 Preheat the oven to 350°F. In a Dutch oven, heat the oil over high. Add the chicken and cook, until browned. Add the onions and let cook for 5 minutes. Add the mushrooms and cook for another 2 minutes, stirring.

2 Add the green peppers, tomatoes, barley, chicken broth and thyme. Season to taste with salt and pepper and mix well. Bring to a boil.

3 Cover the pot, transfer to the oven and bake for 1 hour, or until the barley is tender and all the liquid is absorbed.

4 Just before serving, garnish with fresh parsley and serve immediately.

Simmered

Chicken à la Basquaise

4 SERVINGS

2 tbsp	olive oil
1	chicken, cut in 8 pieces
	salt and freshly ground pepper, to taste
1 tbsp	paprika
½ cup	julienne-cut cappicola (peppered Italian ham)
2	garlic cloves, thinly sliced
2	onions, thinly sliced
2	green peppers, cut in strips
2	red peppers, cut in strips
1 cup	dry white wine
1 can (14½ oz)	diced tomatoes, drained
1 tsp	chopped fresh thyme
1 tsp	chopped fresh oregano
1	bay leaf

1 Preheat the oven to 350°F. In a Dutch oven, heat the olive oil over medium-high heat. Season the chicken pieces to taste with salt, pepper and dust with paprika, and sauté until golden. Remove and set aside.

2 Add the onions, cappicola and garlic to the pot, and cook, stirring often, for 5 minutes. Add the peppers and cook, stirring often, for another 2 minutes.

3 Add the white wine, tomatoes, thyme, oregano and bay leaf and bring to a boil.

4 Return the chicken pieces to the pot, cover and transfer to the oven. Bake for 45 minutes, until the chicken is cooked through. Serve piping hot with rice or fresh pasta.

Simmered

Orchard Chicken

4 SERVINGS

1 lb	skinless, boneless chicken breast, cut in strips
2 tbsp	all-purpose flour
	salt and freshly ground pepper, to taste
2 tbsp	vegetable oil
2	shallots, chopped
1	garlic clove, chopped
1	apple, peeled, cubed
3 tbsp	chopped fresh parsley
2 tsp	chopped fresh sage
1 cup	apple cider
2 tbsp	Dijon mustard
	sage springs and parsley sprigs (garnish)

1 In large bowl, toss the chicken strips with the flour and season with salt and pepper to taste. In a large nonstick skillet, heat the oil over medium-high heat. Add the chicken and cook, stirring often, until golden.

2 Add the shallots and garlic, lower the heat, and cook, stirring, until the shallots become translucent.

3 Add the apple cubes and the herbs and cook, stirring often, for 3 to 4 minutes, until tender. Meanwhile, whisk together the cider and the mustard.

4 Add the cider mixture to the skillet, increase the heat and bring to a boil. Let simmer, stirring often, until the sauce thickens slightly. Serve garnished with sage and parsley sprigs.

Simmered

Chicken and Dried Plums

6 SERVINGS

1 tbsp	vegetable oil
2 tbsp	butter
12	chicken drumsticks
⅔ cup	orange juice
⅔ cup	chicken broth
	salt and freshly ground pepper, to taste
10 to 15	large dried plums
½ cup	sliced almonds, toasted
	honey, to taste

1 In a large heavy, deep skillet or Dutch oven, heat the oil and melt the butter over high heat. Add the chicken and cook, turning often, until browned.

2 Stir in the orange juice and the broth, and bring to a boil.

3 Season to taste with salt and pepper. Lower the heat, cover and let simmer for 15 minutes. Add the dried plums and almonds.

4 Cover and cook 15 to 20 minutes more, turning the chicken twice, until cooked through. Taste the sauce for seasoning and sweeten with honey as desired. Serve.

Simmered

Arabic Chicken

6 SERVINGS

2 tbsp	olive oil
6 to 8	skinless, boneless chicken thighs
2	medium onions, chopped
3	garlic cloves, chopped
1 tbsp	grated fresh ginger
1	lime, sliced
	juice of 1 lime
1 tsp	saffron or ground turmeric
½ tsp	ground cumin
	pinch ground cinnamon
	celery salt, to taste
	freshly ground pepper, to taste
2½ cups	chicken broth
½ cup	finely chopped fresh parsley
⅓ cup	finely chopped fresh coriander
⅔ cup	sliced pitted green or black olives

1 In a Dutch oven, heat the oil over medium-high heat. Add the chicken thighs, sprinkle with the onions, garlic and ginger, and cook, stirring often, until the chicken is lightly browned.

2 Add the lime slices, lime juice and spices, and season to taste with celery salt and pepper.

3 Pour in the chicken broth and bring to a boil. Lower the heat, cover and let simmer for 25 to 30 minutes, or until the chicken is cooked through.

4 Add the fresh herbs and olives during the final minutes of cooking, mix well and serve with a vegetable couscous.

Simmered

Fiesta Chicken Soup

4 SERVINGS

2 cups	cubed cooked chicken
6 cups	chicken broth
½ tsp	celery seeds
½ tsp	coarse-ground black pepper
2	garlic cloves, sliced thinly
1 can (28 oz)	tomatoes, drained and cubed
1	green pepper, cut into cubes
1	onion, chopped
2 tbsp	chopped fresh cilantro or parsley
½ tsp	ground cumin
½ tsp	crushed red pepper
	salt to taste
1¼ cups	frozen or drained canned corn niblets
4	green onions, sliced thinly
1 cup	cooked white rice

Garnish

2 tbsp	chopped fresh parsley
	corn chips
1 cup	grated white cheddar cheese

1 In a large heavy saucepan, combine the chicken, the broth, garlic, celery seeds and black pepper. Bring to a boil over high heat. Lower the heat, cover and let simmer for 30 minutes.

2 Add the tomatoes, green pepper, onion, cilantro or parsley, cumin and the crushed red pepper. Season with salt and let simmer for 10 minutes, until the vegetables are tender.

3 Add the corn, green onions and the rice. Cook until the soup boils and the corn is tender. Remove from the heat.

4 Ladle the soup into ovenproof bowls, and garnish with the cheddar and chopped parsley. Melt the cheese under the broiler, if desired. Serve with corn chips.

Simmered

Spicy Chicken

4 SERVINGS

3 tbsp	vegetable oil
2 tbsp	curry powder
2 tbsp	chopped fresh oregano
1 tbsp	ground cumin
1 tsp	ground cayenne pepper
1	garlic clove, chopped
1	chicken, cut into 8 pieces **(3¼–3½ lb)**
1 can	diced tomatoes in mixed herbs, with juice **(28 oz)**
	salt and freshly ground pepper, to taste

1 In a large bowl, mix together 2 tbsp oil, curry powder, oregano, cumin, cayenne pepper and garlic.

2 Place the chicken in the marinade and turn to coat. Cover and marinate for at least 3 hours in the refrigerator.

3 In a large, deep, nonstick skillet, heat the remaining 1 tbsp oil over medium heat. Add the chicken and cook, turning frequently, until golden.

4 Discard any excess fat, add the tomatoes and bring to a boil. Lower the heat, cover and let simmer for 20 minutes, until the chicken is cooked through. Season to taste with salt and pepper.

Simmered

Poultry Rice Soup

2 SERVINGS

1 can	condensed chicken broth
1 cup	water
¼ cup	long-grain rice
¼ cup	finely chopped green onions
3 tbsp	butter
⅓ cup	all-purpose flour
¼ tsp	dried sage
	salt and freshly ground pepper, to taste
1 cup	light cream
¾ cup	cubed cooked chicken or turkey
2	slices of crisp-cooked bacon, crumbled
2 tbsp	chopped green pepper
2 tbsp	dry sherry (optional)

1 In a heavy saucepan, mix the chicken broth and water. Add the rice and green onions. Bring to a boil over high heat. Lower the heat, cover and let simmer for 20 to 30 minutes or until the rice is tender.

2 In a heavy medium skillet, melt the butter over medium heat. Stir in the flour and sage; season with salt and pepper. Cook for 1 minute, stirring constantly. Gradually add the cream, stirring constantly, until the mixture thickens and boils.

3 Slowly add the cream sauce to the rice mixture while stirring. Add the remaining ingredients. Heat slowly, stirring often; do not boil.

4 Taste for seasoning. Ladle into bowls and serve immediately.

Simmered

Velouté Milanais

8 SERVINGS

4 cups	chicken broth
1 tbsp	butter
2	skinned and boned chicken breast halves
½ cup	julienne-cut ham
1½ cups	sliced mushroom,
3 tbsp	cornstarch
1 cup	light cream
½ cup	tomato purée
¼ cup	grated parmesan cheese
	salt and freshly ground pepper, to taste

1 In a large heavy saucepan, bring the chicken broth to a boil. Cover and keep warm.

2 Melt the butter in a large nonstick skillet over medium heat. Cook the chicken, turning once, for 8 minutes, until cooked through. Remove and set aside. Add the mushrooms and ham to the skillet, sauté for 5 minutes.

3 Whisk the cornstarch into the cream. Return broth to medium heat. Whisk in cornstarch mixture and tomato purée. Cook, stirring, until thickened and bubbly.

4 Cut the chicken into fine julienne. Add the chicken, ham and mushrooms to the broth Season to taste with salt and pepper and heat through. Ladle into bowls and sprinkle with parmesan.

Note
An ideal addition to soups and sauces, heavy or country cream has the same consistency as 35% cream, but with only 15% butterfat.

Simmered

Caribbean Chicken

8 SERVINGS

3 lb	skinless, boneless chicken breast and/or thighs, cut in cubes
	freshly ground black pepper, to taste
	ground cayenne pepper, to taste
2	garlic cloves, chopped
	juice of 2 lemons
2 tbsp	curry powder
3 tbsp	vegetable oil
2	onions, thinly sliced
2 cups	water
1½ tsp	chopped fresh parsley
	pinch of ground thyme
	pinch of ground sage
1	small eggplant, cut in pieces
4	small green onions, chopped
1 tbsp	tomato paste
2	medium potatoes, peeled and cubed or sliced in rounds
1	zucchini, sliced in rounds
	salt to taste
	juice of 1 lemon
1	garlic clove, chopped

1 Season the chicken to taste with black and cayenne pepper and rub with the garlic and lemon juice. Sprinkle with the curry powder. In a large, deep nonstick skillet, heat the oil over medium-high heat. Add the chicken and onions and cook, turning often, until well browned.

2 Add the parsley, thyme and sage, and bring to a boil. Lower the heat, cover and let simmer for 20 minutes.

3 Add the eggplant, green onions and tomato paste, cover and cook another 5 minutes.

4 Add the potatoes, zucchini and salt to taste. Cover and simmer, stirring occasionally, for 10 to 20 minutes more, until the vegetables are tender. Just before serving, sprinkle with the lemon juice and stir in the garlic.

Simmered

Tarragon Chicken

4 SERVINGS

1	small chicken, cut in 8 pieces
	cold water
3	carrots, sliced
2	white parts of leeks, coarsely chopped
½	onion, sliced thinly
2 tbsp	chopped fresh or 1 tsp dried tarragon
1	bay leaf
1	whole clove
	a few sprigs of fresh parsley
2 tbsp	cornstarch, mixed with 3 tbsp cold water
1 cup	plain yogurt
1 cup	sour cream
	salt and freshly ground pepper, to taste

1 Place the chicken in a large heavy saucepan, cover with cold water, cover and bring to a boil over high heat. Remove the chicken and set aside 2 cups of the liquid.

2 Return the chicken to the saucepan, add the vegetables, herbs and spices, the reserved liquid, and enough additional water to cover ¾ of the chicken. Bring to a boil over high heat. Lower the heat, cover and let simmer for 1 hour. Remove the chicken from the saucepan and keep warm.

3 Strain the cooking liquid, and set aside the vegetables. Return the cooking liquid to the saucepan* and heat over low heat. Stir in the cornstarch mixture, yogurt and sour cream, and heat, stirring, until thickened. Do not boil. Season to taste. Discard the bay leaf and clove.

4 Serve the chicken coated with the sauce. Accompany with the vegetables.

Note

* Chill the broth beforehand if you want it to be less fatty. Once chilled, it will be easier to remove any fat that forms on top. If you are in a rush, place a paper towel on the surface of the broth to absorb part of the fat.

Simmered

Mazatlan Chicken and Beans
(Chili Con Pollo de Mazatlan)

6 SERVINGS

2 cups	dried black beans, sorted and rinsed, soaked overnight and drained
10 cups	water
1 tsp	ground black pepper
¼ cup	olive oil
1	red onion, chopped
2	celery stalks, chopped
1	red pepper, chopped
1	white part of leek, chopped
2	jalapeno peppers, chopped
2	garlic cloves, chopped
2 tbsp	chopped fresh oregano or ½ tsp dried oregano
¼ cup	corn flour or corn meal
1 tsp	ground cayenne pepper
1 tsp	ground cumin
2 tbsp	ground coriander
½ tsp	sugar
	salt and freshly ground pepper, to taste
4 cups	chicken broth
1 can (14¾ oz)	creamed corn
4 cups	cubed cooked chicken,
	sour cream (garnish)
	chopped fresh cilantro or parsley, (garnish)

1 Combine the black beans, water and black pepper in a large saucepan and bring to a boil over high heat. Lower the heat and let simmer for 1½ hours, until the beans are very tender. Drain the beans in a sieve and set aside.

2 Rinse and dry the saucepan. In the same saucepan, heat the oil over medium-high heat. Add the red onion, celery, red pepper, leek, jalapeno peppers, garlic and oregano and cook for 5 to 8 minutes, stirring often, until tender.

3 Add the corn flour or corn meal, coriander, cayenne pepper, cumin and sugar. Season with salt and pepper and cook, stirring, for 5 minutes. Add the chicken broth, creamed corn, beans and chicken, and bring to a boil. Lower the heat and let simmer for 15 minutes, stirring frequently.

4 Serve in deep dishes and garnish with sour cream and fresh cilantro or parsley.

Simmered

Floating Avocado Soup

4 SERVINGS

½ lb	skinned and boned chicken breast halves, cut in julienne strips
4 cups	chicken broth
1	chile pepper, seeded and finely chopped
4	garlic cloves, minced
	salt and freshly ground pepper, to taste
1	ripe avocado, halved peeled, pitted and cut in slices
¼ cup	finely chopped fresh cilantro or parsley

1 In a medium saucepan, bring the chicken strips and the broth to a boil over medium-high heat. Lower the heat and simmer for 5 minutes.

2 Add the chile pepper and garlic and season to taste with salt and pepper. Let simmer for 8 minutes.

3 Place the avocado slices one at a time in the hot soup.

4 When the avocado slices float to the surface, the soup is ready to serve in bowls. Garnish with the cilantro or parsley.

Simmered

Chicken Breasts with Spinach

4 SERVINGS

1 cup	chicken broth
4	skinless, boneless chicken breast halves, approximately 3½ oz each
½	onion, thinly sliced
	leaves of one celery stalk, chopped
1 tbsp	vegetable oil
4	canned artichoke hearts, sliced
2	shallots, chopped
1	garlic clove, chopped
2 cups	chopped fresh spinach
	salt and freshly ground pepper, to taste
1 tsp	dried tarragon
2 tsp	cornstarch, mixed with 1 tbsp cold water

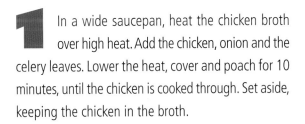

1 In a wide saucepan, heat the chicken broth over high heat. Add the chicken, onion and the celery leaves. Lower the heat, cover and poach for 10 minutes, until the chicken is cooked through. Set aside, keeping the chicken in the broth.

2 In a large nonstick skillet, heat the oil over medium-high heat and add the shallots, artichoke hearts, garlic and spinach. Season to taste with salt and pepper and sprinkle with the tarragon. Cook, stirring, for 2 minutes, until the vegetables are tender.

3 Garnish the bottom of a serving dish with the spinach mixture, slice the chicken breasts and arrange decoratively on top.

4 Stir the cornstarch mixture into the chicken broth. Bring to a boil over medium heat, stirring until thickened. Ladle over the chicken and vegetables and serve.

Simmered

Chicken Ragout

4 SERVINGS

1 cup	dried white beans
	cold water
3 tbsp	butter
1 lb	skinless, boneless chicken thighs
	salt and freshly ground pepper, to taste
2	celery stalks, thinly sliced
2	carrots, sliced into thin rounds
1	onion, chopped
½ cup	brown rice
3 cups	chicken broth
2 tsp	chopped fresh parsley

1 In a medium saucepan, cover the beans with cold water. Bring to a boil over high heat and let boil for 2 minutes. Remove from the heat, cover, and let stand for 1 hour.

2 Preheat the oven to 300°F. Drain the beans and place in a Dutch oven.

3 In a large nonstick skillet, melt the butter over medium-high heat. Add the chicken, season with salt and pepper and cook, stirring often, until browned.

4 Place the chicken and pan juices in the Dutch oven. Add all the other ingredients and bring to a boil over high heat. Cover, place in the oven and bake for 4 hours or until the beans are very tender. Taste for seasoning and serve.

Simmered

Chicken Paella

4 SERVINGS

1 tbsp	olive oil
½ lb	skinless, boneless chicken breast, cubed
1 cup	long-grain rice
1	medium onion, chopped
1	garlic clove, sliced thinly
1½ cups	chicken broth
1 cup	crushed canned tomatoes with their juice
1 tsp	paprika
½ lb	medium shrimp, shelled and deveined
1	red pepper, cut in strips
1	green pepper, cut in strips
½ cup	frozen green peas
	salt and freshly ground pepper, to taste

1 In a large heavy saucepan, heat the oil over high heat. Add the chicken cubes and cook, stirring often, until browned.

2 Stir in the rice, onion and garlic, and cook, stirring often, until the onion is tender and the rice slightly browned.

3 Add the chicken broth, tomatoes and paprika. Bring to a boil, lower the heat, cover and cook slowly, for 10 minutes.

4 Add the shrimp, peppers and peas. Season to taste with salt and pepper and cook covered for 10 minutes, or until the rice is tender and the liquid is absorbed. Serve hot.

Simmered

Chicken Waterzoï

4 SERVINGS

3 tbsp	butter
3	carrots, sliced
2	white parts of leeks, sliced
3	celery stalks, sliced
1	small chicken, cut into 8 pieces
1	chicken liver, coarsely chopped
1	bay leaf
1	sprig of fresh thyme
8 cups	chicken broth
4	egg yolks
1 cup	heavy cream
4	slices of crusty bread
	salt and freshly ground pepper, to taste

1 In a Dutch oven, melt 2 tbsp butter over medium heat. Add the vegetables and cook, stirring often, for 5 minutes. Add the chicken and liver, and cook, turning often, for 15 minutes. Add the herbs and broth; increase the heat and bring to a boil. Lower the heat and simmer, covered, for 90 minutes.

2 In a medium bowl, beat the egg yolks together with the cream; set aside. Cut the bread slices in half. Melt the remaining 1 tbsp butter in a skillet over medium heat and brown the bread in the butter.

3 Remove the chicken and vegetables, and keep warm. Discard the bay leaf and thyme. Whisk the cream mixture with a little hot broth to warm it, then transfer to the broth, whisking well. Return the chicken and vegetables to the sauce to reheat gently.

4 Season to taste with salt and pepper, and serve accompanied with the croutons.

Simmered

Chicken Sausage Rigatoni

4 SERVINGS

½ lb	Italian-style chicken or turkey sausages
2 tbsp	olive oil
1 cup	cubed unpeeled eggplant
1	red pepper, cubed
1	green pepper, cubed
1	garlic clove, chopped
2 cups	diced canned tomatoes with their juice
½ tsp	dried basil
½ tsp	dried oregano
½ tsp	dried thyme
	salt and freshly ground pepper, to taste
½ lb	rigatoni
2 tbsp	fresh oregano leaves (garnish)

1 Cut the sausages into 1-in. pieces. Place them in a large nonstick skillet and simmer uncovered in ¼ cup of water over medium-high heat. Let the water evaporate, and then lightly brown the sausages in 1 tbsp of the olive oil.

2 Add the eggplant and the remaining 1 tbsp olive oil and cook over medium heat for 15 minutes, stirring occasionally. Add the peppers and garlic, and cook another 3 minutes.

3 Stir in the tomatoes and dried herbs. Crush the tomatoes with the back of a spoon and let simmer uncovered for 5 minutes. Season to taste with salt and pepper.

4 Meanwhile, cook the rigatoni until al dente in a large pot of boiling salted water. Drain and mix with the sausage mixture in a large warm bowl. Garnish with fresh oregano and serve immediately.

Note
Chicken sausage is sometimes fully cooked, needing only to be browned and heated through.

Simmered

Greek-style Chicken-stuffed Pita

4 SERVINGS

1 lb	ground chicken
⅓ cup	plain dry bread crumbs
1	egg
2 tbsp	milk
2 tbsp	lemon juice
½ tsp	dried mint
½ tsp	dried oregano
	salt and freshly ground pepper, to taste
1 tbsp	vegetable oil
¼ cup	mayonnaise
2	pita breads, cut in half crosswise
4	slices of red onion
4	tomato slices
8	cucumber slices

1 In a medium bowl, mix together the ground chicken, bread crumbs, egg, milk, 1 tbsp of lemon juice, mint and oregano, and season to taste with salt and pepper.

2 Shape this mixture into patties. Heat the oil in a large nonstick skillet over medium heat, or preheat the broiler. Pan-fry or broil the patties, turning once, for approximately 8 minutes.

3 In a small bowl, mix together the mayonnaise and the remaining 1 tbsp lemon juice. Spoon some sauce into each pita pocket half and place one chicken patty in each.

4 Fill the pitas with the slices of red onion, tomato and cucumber. Serve.

Note

You can replace the mayonnaise with plain yogurt seasoned with chopped garlic.
Do you often eat on the run? Why not take along this super-quick chicken burger? Treat yourself to a delicious meal that is quickly prepared!

In Sandwiches

Chicken Sandwich
with Toasted Almonds

4 SERVINGS

8	slices of crusty country-style bread
1½ cups	chopped cooked chicken
½ cup	mayonnaise
¼ cup	sliced almonds, toasted
½	celery stalk, chopped
2 tbsp	chopped red onion
2 tbsp	chopped fresh chives
1 tbsp	Dijon mustard
	salt and freshly ground pepper, to taste

1 Toast the bread slices.

2 In a medium bowl, mix together all the other ingredients. Season to taste with salt and pepper.

3 Spread 4 slices of toast with the mixture and top each with a slice of toast.

4 Serve accompanied with a small salad, dressed with lemon juice and fruity olive oil.

In Sandwiches

Chicken-Burger Surprise

4 SERVINGS

1 lb	ground chicken
2 tbsp	paprika
1 tbsp	curry powder
½ tsp	dried oregano
½ tsp	dried thyme
	cayenne pepper, to taste
	salt and freshly ground black pepper, to taste
1 tbsp	butter
4	hamburger buns, toasted
4	slices of cheddar or Swiss cheese
4	leaves of lettuce

1 In a medium bowl, mix together the ground chicken, paprika, curry powder, oregano, thyme and season to taste with cayenne pepper, salt and black pepper.

2 Shape into 4 patties and set aside.

3 In a large nonstick skillet, melt the butter over medium heat. Cook the patties for 5 to 7 minutes on each side, until cooked through.

4 Place the chicken patties in the toasted buns, and top with the cheese and lettuce.

In Sandwiches

Tex-Mex
Chicken Sandwich

4 SERVINGS

4	6-in. flour tortillas
½ cup	home-made or prepared salsa, plus extra for serving
1½ cups	cubed cooked chicken
1	avocado, halved, peeled, pitted, and cubed
1	thinly sliced yellow pepper
½ cup	thinly sliced red onion
1 cup	grated Monterey Jack cheese
¼ cup	sour cream

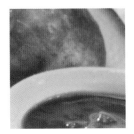

1 Preheat the broiler. Place the tortillas on 2 baking sheets and spread each with some salsa. Top with the chicken and vegetables.

2 Sprinkle each tortilla with ¼ cup of the cheese.

3 Broil, in batches, 4 to 6 in. from the heat for 3 to 5 minutes, until the cheese is well browned, and the vegetables and chicken are heated. Remove the tortillas from the oven.

4 Serve with the sour cream and additional salsa. Accompany with a green salad.

In Sandwiches

Double Meat Croissants

4 SERVINGS

4	croissants
2	skinless, boneless chicken breast halves sliced and cooked
4½ oz	slices cooked ham
12	spinach leaves, blanched
1 cup	prepared white sauce (from a mix)
1 cup	grated Swiss cheese

1 Preheat the broiler. Cut the croissants in half lengthwise. Place the bottom halves on a baking sheet.

2 Arrange the sliced chicken, ham and spinach leaves on the croissant bottoms. Wrap the upper parts of the croissants in foil. Place on a lower oven rack to warm.

3 Spoon the white sauce over each croissant bottom and sprinkle each with some grated cheese.

4 Broil the croissants 4 to 6 in. from the heat for 3 to 5 minutes, until hot and bubbly. Cover with the croissant tops. Serve.

Note
You can buy pre-cooked chicken or broil, poach or pan-fry the chicken breasts.

In Sandwiches

Oriental Burger

4 SERVINGS

½ **lb**	lean ground beef
1 cup	bean sprouts (optional)
¼ **cup**	grated parmesan cheese
1	egg, beaten
1 tbsp	sesame seeds
2 tbsp	chopped fresh chives or chopped green onion
1 tbsp	beef broth granules
4	4 oz pre-made fresh chicken burgers
1 tbsp	toasted sesame oil
4	hamburger buns, toasted

1 Preheat the broiler. In a medium bowl, combine the ground beef, bean sprouts, if using, cheese, sesame seeds, egg, chives and beef broth granules. Mix well.

2 Shape into 4 patties measuring 4½ in. in diameter and press them together with the chicken burgers, brushing with the sesame oil.

3 Broil for approximately 5 minutes each side, until cooked through. Place the patties into the toasted buns.

4 Garnish to taste with sliced tomatoes and lettuce and serve.

Note
For a different version, omit the ground beef and replace with a vegetable such as grated carrots or grated cabbage.

In Sandwiches

Chicken Tacos

4 SERVINGS

2 tbsp	vegetable oil
1 lb	thin chicken breast slices, cut in strips
	salt and freshly ground black pepper, to taste
1	green pepper, cut in strips
1	red pepper, cut in strips
1	onion, thinly sliced
1	garlic clove, chopped
1 jar (16 oz)	salsa
2 tbsp	chopped fresh parsley
8	taco shells, heated

Garnish

shredded lettuce

guacamole

sour cream

1 In a large heavy skillet, heat the oil over high heat. Add the chicken, season to taste with salt and pepper and cook, tossing often, until browned.

2 Add the peppers, onion and garlic, and lower the heat to medium. Continue cooking, stirring often, for 4 minutes, until the vegetables are tender.

3 Stir in the salsa and let simmer for 5 minutes. Remove from the heat and add the chopped parsley.

4 Fill the taco shells with this mixture. Garnish with lettuce, guacamole and sour cream. Serve.

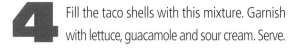

In Sandwiches

Tasty Chicken Burgers

4 BURGERS

1 lb	ground chicken
1	egg, beaten
¼ cup	chopped onion
¼ cup	plain dry bread crumbs
2 tbsp	chopped fresh parsley
1 tbsp	chicken broth granules
	salt and freshly ground pepper, to taste
4	hamburger buns, toasted
	lettuce, in strips
4	tomato slices
	thinly sliced green onions
	mayonnaise

1 Preheat the barbecue grill to medium-hot. In a large bowl, thoroughly mix together the ground chicken, egg, onion, bread crumbs, parsley, chicken broth granules and salt and pepper.

2 Shape this mixture into four patties.

3 Grill the burgers for approximately 10 minutes, turning once, until cooked through.

4 Serve on the toasted buns, garnished with lettuce, tomatoes and green onions and spread with mayonnaise.

In Sandwiches

Baguettes Surprise

4 SERVINGS

1 tbsp	butter
1 lb	ground chicken
1	onion, chopped
¼ cup	prepared barbecue sauce
2	thin crusty baguettes or submarine buns, halved lengthwise
2	tomatoes, sliced
8	cheese slices, any kind
1 tsp	paprika

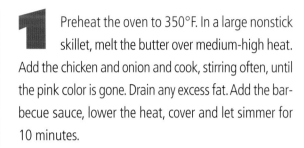

1 Preheat the oven to 350°F. In a large nonstick skillet, melt the butter over medium-high heat. Add the chicken and onion and cook, stirring often, until the pink color is gone. Drain any excess fat. Add the barbecue sauce, lower the heat, cover and let simmer for 10 minutes.

2 Spread the meat mixture over each bread half, place on a baking sheet and bake for 10 minutes, until heated and bubbly.

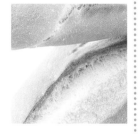

3 Remove from the oven and top with the tomato slices and cheese. Dust lightly with paprika. Return to the oven to brown and melt the cheese.

4 Serve immediately, accompanied with a salad or crudités.

Note

For very tasty baguettes, you can add peppers, hard-boiled eggs … just let your imagination lead the way!

In Sandwiches

Tex-Mex Peppers

4 SERVINGS

4	large green or red peppers
1 lb	cooked white chicken meat, finely chopped or shredded
1	carrot, finely chopped
½ cup	grated gruyère or Swiss cheese
1	jalapeno pepper, seeded and thinly sliced
5	pitted black olives, chopped

Sauce

½ cup	plain yogurt
¼ cup	mayonnaise
	juice of 1 lime
1	green onion, chopped
2	garlic cloves, chopped
1 dash	Tabasco sauce
	salt and freshly ground pepper, to taste

1 Slice the tops off the peppers. Clean them carefully, and steam for 5 minutes (they must remain firm). Chill in the refrigerator.

2 In a medium bowl, mix together the chicken, carrot, cheese, jalapeno pepper and olives.

3 Prepare the sauce by mixing all the ingredients together in a small bowl. Pour the sauce over the chicken mixture and mix well.

4 Stuff the peppers with the chicken mixture and chill until ready to serve.

Note
This dish is served chilled and keeps well in a lunchbox if you also include a can of frozen juice (which preserves the freshness of the items in the lunchbox).

Little Surprises

Chicken Ravioli with Pesto

4 SERVINGS

Pesto Tomato Sauce

1 tbsp	vegetable oil
2 tbsp	chopped onion
1 tsp	chopped fresh garlic
1 can (28 oz)	diced tomatoes in mixed herbs
2 tbsp	prepared pesto
1 tbsp	tomato paste
	salt and freshly ground pepper, to taste
2 packages (9 oz each)	fresh chicken ravioli
2 tbsp	grated parmesan cheese, for serving

1 In a heavy medium saucepan, heat the oil over medium heat. Lightly sauté the onion and garlic. Add the tomatoes, pesto and tomato paste and season to taste with salt and pepper. Bring to a boil. Lower the heat and let simmer for 15 to 20 minutes, until thickened. Keep warm.

2 Cook the ravioli in a large pot of boiling salted water until they are tender and float to the surface. Drain in a colander and transfer to a large, warmed serving bowl.

3 Rewarm the sauce, if necessary, and taste for seasoning, adding more pesto if desired.

4 Spoon the sauce over the ravioli and sprinkle with parmesan. Serve additional parmesan at the table.

Little Surprises

Steamed Chicken Dumplings

36 DUMPLINGS

½ lb	ground chicken
⅓ cup	thinly sliced water chestnuts
⅓ cup	thinly sliced mushrooms
2 tbsp	thinly sliced green onions
1	egg yolk
⅓ cup	cornstarch
2 tbsp	light corn syrup
1 tbsp	soy sauce
1 tsp	vegetable oil
1 tsp	thinly sliced fresh ginger
1	garlic clove, sliced thinly
36	won ton wrappers

Soy Sauce Dip

½ cup	soy sauce
¼ cup	light corn syrup
¼ cup	rice vinegar
1 tbsp	cornstarch
¼ to ½ tsp	crushed red pepper

1 In a medium bowl, combine the ground chicken, water chestnuts, mushrooms, green onions and egg yolk. Add the cornstarch, corn syrup, soy sauce, oil, ginger and garlic. Mix well. Cover and refrigerate for 1 hour.

2 Place 1 tsp of the mixture in the center of each won ton wrapper. Fold the corners in to the center, without closing. Place the dumplings in a flat steamer basket or on a rack over a large saucepan of boiling water.

3 Cover and steam, in batches if necessary, for 20 minutes, or until the dumplings are firm and the chicken is cooked.

4 Meanwhile, in a small saucepan, combine all the dip ingredients. Bring to a boil over medium-high heat, stirring constantly; let boil for 1 minute to thicken. Reheat the dumplings if required, and serve with this dip.

Little Surprises

Small Turkey Roast with Honey, Soy and Sesame Seeds

2 to 4 SERVINGS

1 lb	turkey breast fillet
¼ cup	honey
2 tbsp	soy sauce
¼ cup	sesame seeds
	salt and freshly ground pepper, to taste
1 tbsp	canola oil

1 Marinate the turkey in the honey and soy sauce in a glass baking dish or zip top plastic bag for 24 hours in the refrigerator.

2 Preheat the oven to 325°F. Drain the turkey, coat with the sesame seeds, and season to taste with salt and pepper.

3 Heat the oil in a large nonstick ovenproof skillet over medium heat. Brown the turkey on both sides in the skillet then place in the oven. Bake for 12 to 15 minutes without turning, until cooked through.

4 Remove from the oven and slice and serve hot or cold with vegetables or a salad, or a mustard vinaigrette with dried tomatoes.

Little Surprises

Index

Notes
